The Heart of Our Music

The Heart of Our Music
Underpinning Our Thinking

*Reflections on Music and Liturgy
by Members of the Liturgical Composers Forum*

edited by John Foley

LITURGICAL PRESS
Collegeville, Minnesota

www.litpress.org

Publication of this work was made possible in part by a gift in memory of Kathleen M. O'Brien, a dedicated student of liturgy and an accomplished liturgical musician who practiced her ministry in Washington, DC, and at US Air Force bases throughout the world in partnership with her husband John L. O'Brien.

© 2015 by Order of Saint Benedict, Collegeville, Minnesota. All rights reserved. No part of this book may be reproduced in any form, by print, microfilm, microfiche, mechanical recording, photocopying, translation, or by any other means, known or yet unknown, for any purpose except brief quotations in reviews, without the previous written permission of Liturgical Press, Saint John's Abbey, PO Box 7500, Collegeville, Minnesota 56321-7500. Printed in the United States of America.

1   2   3   4   5   6   7   8   9

Library of Congress Control Number: 2015932167

ISBN 978-0-8146-4851-3   ISBN 978-0-8146-4876-6 (ebook)

Contents

Preface vii
John Foley, SJ

1. A Sacrifice of Praise: Musical Composition as *Kenosis* 1
Alan J. Hommerding

2. "The Word Is Near You, in Your Mouth and in Your Heart": Music as Servant of the Word 10
Bob Hurd

3. The Songs We Sing: The Two Languages of Worship 25
Tony Barr

4. Moving to *Metamelos*: A New Heart, a New Church, a New Song 34
Rory Cooney

5. Beauty and Suitability in Music in the Liturgy 44
Paul Inwood

6. From "God, Beyond All Names" to "O Agape": Images of God in Liturgical Music 58
Jan Michael Joncas

List of Contributors 84

Credits 86

Preface

Sixteen composers of the wonderful music we sing at mass have written essays for this series entitled *The Heart of Our Music*. All of these writers are also ministers of the liturgy, and in these chapters they disclose the experience and wisdom that lie beneath liturgy and their ritual music.

The essays are thought-provoking and written for everyone interested in liturgy—especially those concerned with pastoral music in the English-speaking world. This includes pastors, deacons, liturgists, musicians, ministers of the liturgy, people in the pews, and last, but definitely not least, those interested in the future of Christian worship. The authors have devoted their lives to furthering liturgy, because it is the "fount and apex of the whole Christian life."[1]

This series is a product of discussions and sharings at yearly meetings of the Liturgical Composers Forum in St. Louis. I had the good fortune to establish this forum in 1998, and I was privileged to oversee it until 2011 as part of my work as director of the Center for Liturgy at St. Louis University. Since stepping down from that position I have remained a happy member of the Forum, now incorporated on its own.[2]

In this first volume, "Underpinning Our Thinking," the reader will find reflections on liturgy and composition—first as an "emptying" or "kenosis" (Alan J. Hommerding); then as sacred (Bob Hurd); as actively inviting and challenging us (Tony Barr); as a turning away from "empire" (Rory Cooney); as "good" in the proper sense (Paul Inwood); and as imaging God (Jan Michael Joncas).

How could a short volume be more interesting? I warmly invite the reader to the feast. Come into *The Heart of Our Music*!

—John Foley, SJ

Notes

1. *Lumen Gentium* 11; cf. *Catechism of the Catholic Church* 1324.

2. Membership in the Liturgical Composers Forum consists of persons who have composed a representative body of ritual vocal music that is (1) published by a recognized publisher of liturgical music, (2) intended primarily for the Roman Catholic liturgy, and (3) rooted in participation by the assembly.

1

A Sacrifice of Praise
Musical Composition as *Kenosis*

Alan J. Hommerding

Music was a prominent part of first-century Jewish prayer life. It was a feature of the daily rhythms of Jewish households and the communities they formed. Yet contrasted with other aspects of the life of Jesus such as table fellowship, there is hardly any mention of music in the accounts we have of his life. To be precise, there are three.

One of these is found at Luke 15:25. It is part of the return of the prodigal son. The older, faithful son, who has been laboring dutifully in the field, returns from the fields to the sounds of music and dancing. In other words, somebody got a party started in his absence—not for him, the faithful, dutiful, laboring, sweaty one, but for his greedy, carefree, abandoning, pig-reeking brother. Luke uses the music here to signal a feast being thrown for the least likely guest of honor.

Interesting. But the other two instances serve the purpose of this chapter even better.

In their accounts of the Last Supper both Mark (14:26) and Matthew (26:30) describe Jesus and his followers singing a psalm while they go from the Upper Room to the Mount of Olives. The description is one lone sentence between Jesus' prediction of his own dying and rising, and the prediction of Peter's denial. In the larger literary structure it concludes the narrative of the supper where Jesus identifies himself with the bread and wine. This sentence inaugurates the narrative that will lead to the crucifixion on Calvary, where Jesus will surrender himself, body and spirit, on the cross.

I like to refer to psalm singing in these Last Supper accounts as a "kenotic hinge" used by Matthew and Mark. The act of singing praise to God is simultaneously an act of emptying one's body of breath, which was used by the Creator to animate clay into humanity, and an act of emptying one's spirit in worship. It is this psalm-singing, this musical act of self-emptying, placed by Mark and Matthew between the two great acts of Jesus pouring himself out, that can form a basis for composers to understand their ministry as an act of self-emptying.

Kenosis: The Self-Emptying of Jesus Christ

A basic definition of kenosis is the self-emptying activity that Jesus Christ chose as a means to take on human nature. Appropriately enough, its locus in the New Testament is in a hymn text: Paul's great hymn found in Philippians 2:3-11.

In using the term, however, a few cautions must be expressed. Kenosis does not mean that Jesus Christ stopped being God, that his divine attributes ceased. Nor does it mean merely that he took on mortal flesh and human nature, as crucial as that is. It also expresses why he did so. Verses seven and eight, the critical verses, describe the purpose of this incarnation as threefold: (a) to become human, (b) to be humbled as a servant (or slave), and (c) to be obedient to death on the cross. This is the goal of the kenosis. It precedes the re-exaltation that begins in verse nine. One might say that the destiny of Christ's self-emptying was his self-sacrifice.

Paul and subsequent theologians were grappling with a mystery, kenosis, attempting to describe what is indescribable, to explain what is inexplicable. In a similar way, the Council of Trent used the term "transubstantiation" as being "a most apt" (*aptissime*) way to describe what happens to the eucharistic elements at Mass. Neither term is a complete explanation of these mysteries—a goal beyond our mortal abilities. I include the analogy to Trent because I will place the kenotic dynamic as it pertains to the work of composers into some eucharistic contexts.

Composers have a role in the ongoing creative activity of God through compositions and particular gifts bestowed by the Spirit. But the music we write does not consist of "things" that God has placed in us that we subsequently share with others so that they, too, can access a portion of God. Such an understanding does not contain the sense of surrender that a composer-disciple must be in touch with in order to follow the kenotic, eucharistic call of Jesus Christ.

It is much better to think of ourselves as agents in the ongoing dynamic of revelation actuated by the Holy Spirit, continually recalling this power of the Spirit by which Christ became human as the model for the kenosis of the Spirit in our lives. For this reason, I consciously avoid use of the term "gift" or the expression "self-gift," since our surrounding culture too often identifies our "gifts" (musical or otherwise) as some objective, quantifiable entity we own or possess, with which we (sometimes over-) identify our very selves.

Compositional "Kenosis"—Three Eucharistic Views

Kenosis as Identity: The Last Supper

"Take and sing" or "Take and play," the composer might say when offering a new piece of music. It must be admitted that composers inevitably identify the compositions they create with themselves. This is understandable and, to a certain extent, a good thing, for it is one aspect of care or concern about one's musical craft. It is no accident that composers often use expressions such as "a part of me" or "like my children" to refer to the intimate degree to which they identify with the music they write. Our musical compositions are "my pieces" in more ways than one.

But if composers truly take Christ as their model for self-emptying, a next step would be to recall Christ offering himself in bread and cup "for you" and doing so freely, out of love. For the composer to say in a Christlike fashion that something he or she has written is "for you" (whether that "you" is another musician, a local community, or the wider church) does not mean that the composer is motivated by some sort of personal benefit but is truly offering music out of a desire to benefit others. This is true self-emptying, motivated by love. Paul's checklist from 1 Corinthians 13:4-13 is a pretty good set of criteria to evaluate our compositional motivations. Am I patient with how long it's taking the choir to learn "my" new piece? Is it possible I wrote this because I'm jealous of another composer's setting of the same text?

Misinterpretation is the bane of a composer's existence. Most composers can relate to it, especially when and if their works are performed in musical circumstances of which they are not a part. It may be difficult to experience interpretations other than one's own, but the grace of the Spirit can lead us to be freed of that need to control, opening us to the diversity and possibilities that we don't even know exist in our work. Composers need to empty themselves to offer their music freely, as Christ offered himself freely at the table. The gospels reveal that Jesus had a great deal of insight into the shortcomings of his followers, so it is easy enough to imagine that, as he left them his Body and Blood in the elements of their supper so that they could remember him, he could presume that, along with his teachings, these would be used and interpreted in ways that he did not intend. Yet he still offered himself at that meal.

Kenosis as Sacrifice: Calvary

I am not going to reflect on those long hours composers spend striving to perfect our compositions until our eyes are bloodshot and our backs are sore. That sort of bodily sacrifice truly occurs, but a more important sort of sacrifice is the uniting of our work with the saving work of Jesus Christ on Calvary. This happens in a twofold way: the church (including its composers) acting as the baptized Body of Christ, and liturgical prayer being sung with the music that we write for it.

The kenotic dynamic through which God became incarnate continues in baptism. As Paul tells us in Romans 6:3-4, this incorporation joins us to the whole reality of Christ's own embodiment, including his sacrificial death and his resurrection. The implications for composers are important. Baptism has placed us and our particular ministry of composition within the Body of Christ as one of its contributing members. When we compose for the church we are writing music for Christ to sing. Far from being a cause for self-aggrandizement, this reality must return us again and again to the emptying, humbling dynamic of kenosis. Through the power of the Holy Spirit, Christ again and again empties himself, humbles himself, incorporates himself with us in each baptized believer—to literally "make us part of the body."

I am using the word "liturgy" here with its widest sweep: not only the eucharistic celebration, but the other sacramental rites, celebrations, and occasions for prayer in which Christ's people gather together to offer Christ's sacrifice to God. The whole of our sung prayer is all part of one great act of praise and thanksgiving. Everything we intend for the liturgy is written to be part of the act of Christ's sacrifice, which we continue through the power of the Holy Spirit. When it comes to writing music for the church's public, corporate prayer, the act of composition is a self-emptying activity per se. For the composer, as member of the Body of Christ, the destiny of kenosis is truly sacrifice. All is the "sacrifice of praise."

Kenosis as Service: Footwashing

Jesus left us commands at the Last Supper. We do better with "Take and eat" and "Take and drink" than we do with "As I have done for you, so you must do." Some (including this author) have wondered what the church would be like if we also enacted footwashing every time we celebrated the Lord's Supper. We must find numerous practical ways to imitate this in our ministry as composers.

Many of us function in leader-servant musical roles in our communities. But one aspect of the Johannine account might serve us well for some self-examination. Jesus upsets his followers' preconceived notions and images about him, the Teacher and Lord. He lived out the kenosis of his origin, humbling himself to take on literally the form of a servant. We might do well to take a serious look at what expectations or preconceived notions people have about us as composers. Do they, on whatever level, try to make us a kind of celebrity, one who is celebrated, one who unintentionally takes the place of Christ? To exaggerate, might they think the ability to craft a musical composition means that all musical knowledge in heaven and on earth has been given to us? In terms of self-image, in what ways do we fail to empty ourselves by kenosis, preferring instead to be full of ourselves? Do we set ourselves up as "teacher and lord" when we function as composers, especially when we take "our" music to others?

Composers may be surprised to see the potential for personal and musical growth that self-emptying and setting aside of oneself can accomplish. Do I always write for four-part choir? Why not write for smaller forces to discover how a leaner texture better expresses the text, perhaps thereby serving a wider range of communities with limited resources? Am I always writing in response-verse form? Perhaps a strophic hymn text will challenge me to achieve something new. Can I write a compelling single-line chant melody, or do I always default to 3/4 time with an arpeggiated accompaniment? Am I ignoring a real lack of musical settings for certain texts or moments in our prayer because I would rather turn to texts that have already been set numerous times? What music by another composer do I not particularly care for? Can I revisit it and find therein something positive, something that I might do well to emulate?

Ritual: Knowing and Embodying Musical Kenosis

It is time to talk of ritual, which has something of a bad reputation in our culture, a culture that prizes novelty and informality. And yet so many things in our culture are far more ritualistic than anything we do in church! Think of video games and Top 40 radio, for instance. Through human rituals we both know and embody everything from survival (how to eat) to enjoyment (how to dine). It has been said that God took on our human nature in order to fully understand what it means to be human. This might be considered a bit shortsighted, if not a first step down the heresy trail. God did not necessarily have to grow a head in order to understand what it means to endure a head cold. But still, as Paul's letter to the Hebrews explains more precisely, God did take on our human nature so that *we* would understand that God knows what it means to be fully human. The kenosis that Christ undertook, then, was for this knowing, as well as for his embodiment in human flesh. That embodiment continues to this day through ritual.

The music that composers craft for prayer is a way for the assembly of the baptized to ritualize. Through it people come to experience the larger rhythms of prayer as the words of Holy Scripture are placed in their hearts. They learn when to listen, when to respond, when to participate in an interior mode, and when to give exterior expression. Ritual music is a way to amplify an understanding that the church and its prayer is not a solitary exercise but corporate activity. This is why composers are continually compelled to increase their own understanding of the rites and the prayer of the church. Even if the assembled, baptized faithful could not necessarily articulate their knowledge of the rites, ritual music that is crafted to support and respect the rites will bring them to increased comprehension—and perhaps even appreciation.

Ours is an incarnational religion, one that believes that an immortal being took on mortal flesh; and it is a sacramental religion, one that uses the "stuff" of life—bread, wine, oil, water, women, men—to localize the sacred. I am fond of describing

Christianity as a religion *con carne* and our human bodies as our BSUs (basic sacramental units).

In a way complementary to the "knowing" described above, our liturgical compositions also help the rites to become "incarnate" for those we serve. Through music, people embody the ritual and prayer in a way they otherwise would not. Much research has been done in recent years about the effect of singing on the human brain and body, with the unanimous conclusions that no other human activity engages as much of the brain simultaneously and that the effects of singing include everything from increased levels of proteins and antibodies in the blood to effective allaying of everything from stress to depression.

Of course sacred song and the music we write are not merely about biology, nor is worship merely therapy. Music is a primary way for us to get the rites we pray "into our bones" and pray them "by heart." It is the way we engage others as a thankful, praising assembly of God's faithful. It is the way we enter into dynamic ritual relationship as a community with particular prayer leaders, the way we express our penitence, our joy, our gratitude, and our commitment. Along with posture and environment, ritual and its music are how we continue to be emptied of ourselves and shaped into Christ, sent as we are into the world as that Christ.

Music as an Aural Emblem of the Reign of God

Finally, let us make our way back to Luke's use of music in the parable of the Prodigal Son. At its heart the parable describes one of the most self-emptying figures in all of the gospels: the father who could have had his son killed or enslaved for disobedience, or at the very least could have waited stoically for him to return all the way home. Instead, however, he ignores all social demands, legalities, permissions, and conventions by running out to his son who is far off in the distance. It might be noted that many of Jesus' parables feature a "kenotic" figure like this father.

The return of the son triggers a whole series of "emptyings": the party itself, the emptying of the pantry, the dancing, and the full embodiment and expression of joy. Binding it all together is music. It underscores the feasting, it compels the dancing. In this, as in other gospel depictions of feasts, we are meant to get the smallest glimpse of the great eternal feast of the kingdom, which is our own destiny. Much more than earthly feasts, the heavenly liturgy is an eternal and infinite self-emptying of the hosts of heaven around the throne of the Lamb. And binding it all together is the great canticle of the saints and angels.

Needless to say, this will be the ultimate time of kenosis. Yet it is already mysteriously bound up with us here and now as every knee in heaven, on earth, and under the earth bends at the name of Jesus. This is what calls composers and musicians to serve others, to be, as Charles Wesley expressed it, "lost in wonder, love, and praise."

This reality is what calls composers to kenosis, to self-emptying in our ministry, to setting ourselves aside for the reign of God.

2

"The Word Is Near You, in Your Mouth and in Your Heart"[1]
Music as Servant of the Word

Bob Hurd

What makes sacred music *sacred*?[2] This was a central question guiding *Sing to the Lord*, a rewrite of *Music in Catholic Worship*. Because this question lays bare the nature of worship music it also addresses two other questions. What are music ministers supposed to be doing? What are composers of sacred music supposed to be doing?

The relevant documents give various answers to the "sacredness" question, but at bottom they reveal two types of explanation. One locates the quality of sacredness in the form of the music itself. The other sees music as a "carrier" of a sacredness that comes from elsewhere. This "elsewhere" is the paschal mystery that good music, like good preaching, communicates.[3]

With regard to the first type of explanation, Pius X's 1903 instruction (*Tra le Sollecitudini*) spoke of such attributes as holiness, beauty, and universality and held up Gregorian chant as embodying these qualities.[4] In 1955, Pius XII (*Musicae Sacrae Disciplina*) echoed this, saying sacred music "must be holy," not allowing anything "within itself that savors of the profane."[5] Taken in isolation, such statements seem naïve nowadays. It is extremely difficult to point to this or that quality in a musical piece and say "that's what makes it sacred." Is it the intervals between notes that makes one type "sacred" and another type merely "profane" and bereft of holiness? Is "tempo-less" music (chant) holier than music with meter because the first suggests timelessness and transcendence, while the second anchors us in temporal, earthly existence? But is "rising above the earthly" in this way a truly Christian norm of holiness, given God's embrace of the temporal and the earthly in the incarnation? Or perhaps sacredness derives from the biblical/liturgical text that is sung. But then the first type of explanation (sacredness as something in the music itself) has been abandoned for the second (not in the music, but in the word of God the music "carries").

Before succumbing to such interesting questions, one should notice that even these earlier, pre-Vatican II sources include the second type of explanation. Though Pius X extols Gregorian chant as embodying the quality of sacredness, it is never proposed as the only genre that can do so. He explicitly says that "each country may use in its ecclesiastical music whatever special forms may belong to its own national style" (TLS 2),[6] and he includes the music of Palestrina and "more modern music" as genres that can also embody sacredness (TLS 4–5).[7] Pius XII officially recognized vernacular hymnody or popular religious song as an additional type of sacred music, though he limited its use to low mass. In retrospect, his reason for its suitability is interesting: "these hymns can be a powerful aid in keeping the faithful from attending the Holy Sacrifice like dumb and idle spectators. They can help the faithful accompany the sacred services both mentally and vocally and to join their own piety to the prayers of the priest" (MSD 64).[8]

Since more than one genre can embody the attribute of "sacredness," a norm beyond a particular genre's excellence is implied. What is this norm? Pius X answers this question in describing the role of liturgical music: "since its chief duty is to clothe the liturgical text, which is presented to the understanding of the faithful, with suitable melody, its object is to make the text more efficacious" (TLS 1).[9] On this view, music is sacred because it carries and communicates the sacred text. It is a short step from this to seeing the entire liturgy in all its texts and actions as a sacred text whose enactment may be heightened and rendered more efficacious by music. The Constitution on the Sacred Liturgy, *Sacrosanctum Concilium*, does just that in its oft-quoted statement: "sacred music is to be considered the more holy, the more closely connected it is with the liturgical action" (112). Whether we consider the liturgy as "text" or "action"—in fact it is always both—what is written/enacted is the paschal mystery. To serve the text, to be closely connected to the liturgical action, means *to mediate the paschal mystery*. *Sing to the Lord* expresses this well: "Sacred music is holy when it mediates the holiness of God and forms the Holy People of God more fully into communion with him and with each other in Christ" (69).[10]

But to mediate the paschal mystery well instead of poorly places formal requirements on the music itself. This same paragraph from *Sing to the Lord* speaks of the "inner qualities" of music "that enable it to add greater depth to prayer, unity to the assembly, or dignity to the ritual." In this way, *Sing to the Lord* acknowledges both schools of explanation about the source of sacredness. The point is underscored later in the document's treatment of the three judgments—liturgical, pastoral, and musical—that guide the choice of music for the liturgy: "The musical judgment asks whether this composition has the necessary aesthetic qualities that can bear the weight of the mysteries celebrated in the Liturgy" (134). This phrasing brings together both types of explanation: in order for music to carry or mediate "the mysteries" well, it must embody the "necessary aesthetic qualities."

I would argue, however, that of these two modes of explanation one is more primary. What makes Roman Catholic (and Christian) worship music sacred is, first and theologically speaking, the sacredness of the paschal mystery. As the moon's light is but a reflection of the light of the sun, sacred music's sacredness is a reflection of the glory of the Lord. But in order to fulfill this role as reflector or mediator, music must have the "inner qualities" mentioned above.[11] The beauty and excellence that we want worship music to have "of itself" follows from its role as a servant of something "beyond itself." It is this relation of music to something "beyond itself" that shapes the remainder of this chapter.

Music as Mediator of the Paschal Mystery

Music is sacred insofar as it mediates the paschal mystery. It both communicates this mystery and evokes a profound, heartfelt response on the part of the assembly. It helps to proclaim the Word and brings forth a response—an answering word—of faith and love from worshipers. To show how music does this, let us consider the following question: How is the paschal mystery presented or communicated throughout the text/action of the liturgy?

There are basically two narrative streams that comprise the overall text/action of the liturgy: (1) the Word in the rites and (2) the Word in the readings. The Word in the rites refers to the ritual texts that structure the liturgy and remain relatively fixed from celebration to celebration. By contrast, the Word in the readings—gospel narratives and their accompanying readings—changes with each liturgy. I am using the capitalized "Word" here to cover not only the Liturgy of the Word, but ritual texts, because these, too, are scripturally based. This Word is ultimately the risen Lord himself, who is present to the gathered church through the rites (preeminently the eucharistic prayer) and through the proclamation of the readings. In both narrative streams the assembly encounters the Word, the paschal mystery, Christ himself. And music serves both.[12] In what follows I will first consider how music serves the Word in the rites and then explore its role in relation to the Word in the readings.

Music Mediates the Word in the Rites

Music Interprets Text

Pius X spoke of music's mediating role as making texts more efficacious by clothing them with "suitable melody." How exactly does melody joined to ritual texts such as the *Kyrie* or *Sanctus* do this? Since music itself is not word, it cannot add any new ideational content to the text. So what does it add? Music interprets and heightens the meaning of a text by evoking the feeling and willing that belong to these words. Communion between God and humanity is not only an exchange of information, but primarily formation—a relationship characterized by love, fidelity, solidarity, self-donation, and a whole range of volitional and affective postures. Music expresses this intentionality of the words, the *attitude*, of the text, just as in speech the tone in which we say something helps to determine its meaning. A good melody, like a good actor, renders a text convincingly, giving flesh and blood to the words. A number of melodies and musical genres can authentically render a text, just as many actors can play Hamlet well. In this sense, it is not so much that music adds something as that it actualizes the potential latent in the text.

However, making ritual texts more efficacious is not just a matter of delivering them with conviction to an audience, but rather of enabling the assembly itself to enact them. An audience may participate mentally and profoundly in a text performed by a soloist. But the assembly is supposed to perform the ritual texts of the liturgy both mentally *and* vocally. The form of the music must allow for broad participation. Music mediates ritual texts not only by interpreting them but by allowing the assembly to co-enact the interpretation with its presider and other ministers.

Song—Music and Text Together—Interprets the Rite

Of all the liturgy's ritual texts/actions, the most important is undoubtedly the eucharistic prayer, especially the institution narrative. How do the sung acclamations function in relation to this Word in the rite? A sung *Sanctus* is not only a matter of *this* melody deepening our understanding and enactment of *these* words. But the whole thing, words and music together, interprets the larger rite in which it belongs. Singing the *Sanctus* interprets and discloses the meaning of the preface section of the eucharistic prayer—praise and thanks for God's deeds on our behalf, culminating in the gift and deed of God's only Son. Similarly, at the conclusion of the institution narrative when the text summons us to remember Christ's self-sacrifice for us ("Do this in memory of me"), the memorial acclamation enables the assembly to fulfill this anamnesis by singing the mystery of faith.

To take another example, the Word in the rite of gathering is the renewed identification of the assembling church with the risen Lord and the triune God. By way of a song for the sprinkling rite or a *Kyrie* in the penitential rite, we affirm our bond with Christ. Our praise of the triune God in the *Gloria* discloses that belonging to Christ entails being children of the Father and recipients of Christ's Spirit. Each moment of the rite communicates some aspect of the paschal mystery. The sung text enables the assembly to enact the communication and affirm it in faith. The same applies to the other ritual units of the liturgy, such as the communion rite.

To understand how song interprets rite, we must also consider the role of non-prescribed song-texts. The *Roman Gradual* stipulates antiphons and psalms for gathering, preparation, and Communion. But the *General Instruction of the Roman Missal* also allows non-prescribed songs for these rites (48, 86–88). In fact, non-prescribed songs drawn from a hymnal or worship resource form the bulk of parish music at these moments. How do these songs function in relation to the rite in which they occur? There are basically two possibilities, in line with the two narrative streams of the liturgy. At any given moment in the liturgy, a non-prescribed song will address either the Word in the rite or the Word in the readings. A gathering song that speaks to the action of coming together again as the body of Christ elaborates the Word in the rite. Since what it means to be the body of Christ in the world has many implications—identification with Christ, intimacy with the Father, life in the Spirit, life in solidarity with all of humanity for whom Christ died—gathering texts can expand in many different directions. Similarly, a communion song that explores the meaning of sharing in the body and blood of Christ elaborates the Word in the rite of communion. Consider Bernadette Farrell's "Bread for the World": "May we who eat be bread for others. May we who drink pour out our love."[13] These words underscore the sacrificial dimension of Communion. To share in Christ's body and blood is to enter into his self-emptying for others. Or as Augustine said, in Communion we are to become what we receive. Melody actualizes the potential of a text by bringing out the feeling and willing that belong to its words. Similarly, the song—text and melody together—actualizes the potential of rite by spelling out its various levels of meaning.

The spectrum of textual possibilities in non-prescribed songs includes, on one end, interpreting the rite by quoting scripture (just as the *Roman Gradual* does in its prescribed antiphons/psalms). Contemporary examples are Suzanne Toolan's "I Am the Bread of Life,"[14] and the many settings of Psalm 34, "Taste and See that the Lord is Good." On the other end of the spectrum, a song may draw the assembly into theological reflection, based upon scripture and tradition, but with words created by the composer. Farrell's "Bread for the World," cited above, is a good example, as are older familiar hymns such as "Shepherd of Souls" and "Lord, Who at Thy First Eucharist."

Music Mediates the Word in the Readings

Christ himself "speaks when the Sacred Scriptures are read in Church" says *Sacrosanctum Concilium* (7). One could not ask for a more straightforward affirmation that the Word in the readings mediates Christ to the gathered church. Music that serves this Word is thus an instrument of this conversation between the risen Lord and his church. It is a complex conversation, because the gospel is preceded by a series of other Scriptures, including the psalm and the verse of the gospel acclamation. What is supposed to be happening as we move through this series of texts, culminating in the gospel?

The short answer, given in the Introduction to the *Lectionary for Mass,* is *meditatio:* "The liturgy of the word must be celebrated in a way that fosters meditation" so that the assembly may "take the word of God to heart and prepare a response to it in prayer" (28). What is this response of prayer? Within the Liturgy of the Word it is the intercessions.[15] But considering the liturgy more broadly, the most significant response is the eucharistic prayer. This same dynamic is at the heart of the monastic method of *lectio divina:* we take to heart God's word to us through the Scriptures (*meditatio*) and respond with prayer (*oratio*). In *lectio divina* these two central steps are bookended by two more. *Lectio* (reading) is a first look at a passage of Scripture. It "sets up" the next stage of *meditatio.* The final stage, following *oratio* (prayer) is *contemplatio*, which is wordless communion with the Lord. Parallels between this fourfold structure and the Eucharist are striking. In fact, the Eucharist can be understood as a communal form of *lectio divina*, with music serving as a powerful instrument of the assembly's hearing and responding to the voice of Christ. First, I will consider the Liturgy of the Word as communal *lectio divina*, then widen the scope by seeing the entire liturgy as corresponding to the four stages of *lectio divina.*

The Liturgy of the Word as Communal Lectio Divina

A key element in *lectio divina* is repetition. This also applies to the Liturgy of the Word considered as communal *lectio divina.* M. Basil Pennington describes *meditatio* as carrying "the word within us, repeating it, perhaps even on the lips but certainly in the mind" until it touches the heart and evokes a response.[16] Another helpful image for this is that of an actor learning a script. The actor must rehearse the lines, repeating them over and over, until they sink in. Not only that, but actors also put themselves, their own life experiences, into the script to render it truthfully. There is not only reception *of* but self-donation *to* the script. The Liturgy of the Word is God's script, with Christ as the major character. Christians, who have "put on Christ" in baptism, rehearse and internalize the script so that they may, under Christ's direction, enact his compassion in the world.[17] One of the most important ways in which this repetition, rehearsal, and internalization takes place in the liturgy is through music. The responsorial psalm, for example, is the whole process of *lectio divina* in miniature. The refrain proposes a word or phrase for repetition and memorization; the verses provide variation, supplying insight into different aspects of this Word-refrain, to which we return repeatedly. The combination of repetition and variation or refrain with verses allows us to "chew the cud" of the Word so that it may transform us. By the end of the psalm, the refrain as God's word to us has become our word of reply to God.

But the psalm is only one part within the larger flow of Word. Repetition is at work in this larger flow too, because the psalm usually echoes something in the first reading and anticipates something in the gospel. During the festal seasons (Advent, Christmas, Lent, Easter), the second reading is likewise thematically keyed to the gospel. As the proclamation goes from reading to psalm to reading, there is repetition of themes or images that reemerge in the gospel. So the sung psalm not only interprets its own text, it mediates the unfolding message of the readings culminating in the gospel. This, together with the easily overlooked verse of the gospel acclamation, steers and focuses the assembly's meditation, culminating in the presider's public *meditatio* in the homily. Finally, the Liturgy of the Word is only one part within the overall flow of the liturgy. The widest application of communal *lectio divina* includes the entire liturgy.

The Eucharist as Communal Lectio Divina

How can the whole eucharistic liturgy, from the gathering to the Liturgy of the Word, to the eucharistic prayer, communion rite, and dismissal be understood as a communal form of *lectio divina*? To illustrate this, let us consider the Fourth Sunday of Lent in Year A. After reviewing that Sunday's Scriptures, I will show how the various stages of the liturgy correspond to the four stages of *lectio divina*, and how music may lead the assembly into a progressively deeper encounter with the Word in the readings. The gospel features the cure of the man born blind. The previous readings prepare and focus our meditation on what will emerge in the gospel. In the first reading from 1 Samuel, the prophet anoints the shepherd boy, David—youngest and least of his brothers—as the new king. Psalm 23 echoes the shepherd imagery ("The Lord is my shepherd") as well as the anointing theme ("you anoint my head with oil"). It also describes the Lord strengthening us as we face hostility and danger ("you are at my side / with your rod and your staff / that give me courage"). For when the least is chosen there is likely to be resistance and hostility. The second reading from Ephesians introduces the additional motif of light versus darkness and becoming "children of light." The verse of the gospel acclamation underscores the light theme: "I am the light of the world . . . whoever follows me will have the light of life." All this is revisited/repeated in a new and final way in John's gospel. Jesus, the light of the world, anoints/enlightens one of the least, who, as a child of the light, bears courageous witness before hostile religious authorities. His dawning enlightenment is matched by the Pharisees' deepening resistance and self-inflicted blindness to the light of the world. With the aid of music, the entire liturgy can become a progressive passage into the depths of this Word in the readings.

Gathering as Lectio

Anticipating the day's readings in the gathering rite is no foreign intrusion because one of the gathering rite's aims is to prepare worshipers to hear the Word. By coordinating three moments in the gathering rite, the assembly can be drawn into communal *lectio*—a "first look" at the Word in the readings. A song such as Bernadette Farrell's "Christ Be Our Light" anticipates the light/enlightenment theme.[18] The presider carries this forward, introducing the penitential rite with words such as: "Brothers and sisters, how can we bear witness to the light? Are we not beset by limitations, prejudices, even darkness? Let us turn to the Lord Jesus, who is in our midst. He will show us the way." Third, the invocations of the penitential act may be worded to anticipate the gospel: 1) Lord Jesus, you open our eyes, illumining our darkness: Lord, have mercy. 2) Lord Jesus, you call your church to be a light to the nations: Christ, have mercy. 3) Lord Jesus, you anoint us for discipleship, your word lights the path before us: Lord, have mercy.

Liturgy of the Word as Meditatio

As I said above, the resonance between the readings focuses assembly meditation. Music serves this communal *meditatio* through the responsorial psalm and the alleluia verse. Psalm 23 (The Lord is my shepherd) explicitly links the first reading with what follows. Because of this linking and focusing function, the assigned psalm is normally preferable to a seasonal one. And the alleluia verse is not only acclamatory but proclamatory, since it provides a scriptural encapsulation of the gospel and its enlightenment theme: "I am the light of the world, says the Lord, whoever follows me will have the light of life." As a bridge to the eucharistic prayer, the Taizé-like refrain of Suzanne Toolan's "Jesus Christ, Inner Light," can extend and deepen the assembly's *meditatio* on the Word in the readings: "Jesus Christ, inner light, let not our own darkness conquer us. Jesus Christ, inner light, enable us to welcome your love."[19]

The Eucharistic Prayer as Oratio

The distinction I have made between the Word in the readings and the Word in the rites is not a separation. As *Sing to the*

Lord says, echoing the *General Instruction of the Roman Missal*, "they are so closely connected as to form one act of worship" (28). What ties them together? They both communicate the paschal mystery. The heart of each is Christ himself, who is the Word and the Bread of Life. The Word in the readings tells the paschal story through detailed narratives. The eucharistic prayer retells the same story in its abbreviated essentials, particularly in the institution narrative—the most important narrative moment of the whole liturgy. But it does something more, and this is what distinguishes the Liturgy of the Eucharist from the Liturgy of the Word. Though Christ the Word is truly present in the Word proclaimed, this same Word becomes sacramentally and uniquely present as our food and drink through the eucharistic prayer. That is why the GIRM calls it "the center and summit of the entire celebration" (78). The encounter with Christ, anticipated in the gathering rite and meditated upon in the Liturgy of the Word, reaches its true completion in the eucharistic prayer and communion rite. As mentioned above, within the eucharistic prayer the sung acclamations serve the Word in the rite by engaging the assembly in its meaning and enactment. But all this is done in light of the Word in the readings. We are meant to pray the abbreviated paschal story (the eucharistic prayer) in light of the detailed paschal story (the readings). That is why *The Roman Missal* provides multiple prefaces—so that the eucharistic prayer may be prayed in light of the Word in the readings. The preface for the Fourth Sunday of Lent explicitly echoes the light/darkness and anointing/baptismal motifs of the readings, announcing that Christ came among us to lead us "from darkness into the radiance of faith" and to make us adopted children of God "through the waters of regeneration." What we do at the eucharistic table responds to and completes what we have received at the table of the Word. In this sense, the eucharistic prayer corresponds to the third stage of *lectio divina: oratio* or prayerful response to the Word we have meditated upon in the readings.

The Communion Rite as Contemplatio

The journey traveled so far, from a first look at the Word, to a deeper conversation which makes our hearts burn, to a response of praise, love, and self-donation in prayer, finally brings us to an intimacy with the wordless Word—communion. The Word is now literally "in our mouths" as the Bread of Life. This wordless communion, or *contemplatio*, is paradoxically shaped by many words: the spoken and sung words of the rite, as well as the words of the communion song. This song may elaborate the Word in the rite—that is, the meaning of sharing in the Body and Blood of Christ. But it may, alternatively, mediate the paschal mystery as portrayed in the gospel and other readings. On this Sunday of the man born blind, songs such as Greg Hayakawa's "I Am the Light of the World," Christopher Walker's "Out of Darkness," or Marty Haugen's "Shepherd Me, O God" return us to the Word in the readings.[20] As we are meant to pray the eucharistic prayer in light of the readings, so we may receive the Bread of Life in light of them. Still, all of these words end in silence—not as a rebuff to words, but as their natural endpoint. Word and silence are partners. Words come out of silence and return into it. The communion of lover and beloved ends after many words in their silent presence to each other. Theologically, because Christ is the Word *of God,* nearness to him is nearness to *the* Mystery, something both revealed and concealed, something that is Word but also wordless—the name above all names—the Word above all words!

The parallel between the liturgy and *lectio divina* may be taken further. What comes of intimacy with Christ? *Compassio* and *operatio*. Those who commune with Christ, the very compassion of God poured out on a suffering world, become compassionate with him. What comes of this compassion? *Operatio* or action.[21] Consuming the Eucharist means entering into Christ's self-emptying action for others. The "this" of "Do this in memory of me" is not only the immediate performance of the table-prayer and receiving Communion, but more broadly, the performance of the Christ-script (the Word in the readings) in our lives. Ritually speaking, the dismissal is the natural outcome of the communion rite. To commune with Christ is to be sent forth on mission. On this Sunday, a dismissal song that speaks of mission would not only express generally what it means to commune with Christ (the Word in the rite), but also echo the heart of the gospel story: the Sent One (Christ) anoints another (the blind man), who is in turn sent to bring others to the Light.

What are music ministers and composers of liturgical music supposed to be doing? No more and no less than helping worshipers to hear and respond to the voice of Christ. The Risen One speaks his paschal mystery—his Word of self-emptying love—through the Word in the rite and the Word in the readings. As a mediator of this Word, music prepares the way and makes straight the path. Music ministers and composers labor in the hope that Paul's saying may truly come to pass: "The word is near you, in your mouth and in your heart" (Rom 10:8).

Notes

1. Romans 10:8.
2. *Sing to the Lord: Music in Divine Worship* (Washington, DC: United States Conference of Catholic Bishops, 2007).
3. Edward Foley describes these contrasting explanations as a "functional" versus an "ontological" perception of worship music in *Ritual Music* (Beltsville, MD: The Pastoral Press, 1996) 176–81.
4. TLS 2, cited in Jan Michael Joncas, *From Sacred Song to Ritual Music* (Collegeville, MN: Liturgical Press, 1997), 51. For much of what follows I am indebted to this in-depth study that gathers the pertinent papal and ecclesial statements on music into one place.
5. MSD 42, cited in Joncas, *From Sacred Song to Ritual Music*, 53.
6. Joncas, *From Sacred Song to Ritual Music*, 51.
7. Ibid., 14.
8. Ibid., 17.
9. Ibid., 32.
10. Nos. 67 through 70 discuss the ritual, spiritual, and cultural aspects of liturgical music.

11. This last point is surely a valid principle, even if it is difficult to make aesthetic judgments that do more than betray one's subjective preferences. More humility and less pontificating is required in this quarter. *Sing to the Lord* means well when it criticizes "the musical cliché often found in secular popular songs" (135), but it is an elitist cliché to write off what is popular as inferior. Further, one person's cliché may be another person's musical idiom. Mariachi music may sound like a cliché to persons standing outside Mexican culture, because in their ignorance they notice only what is most obvious. Someone inside the culture knows all the nuances as well as what is obvious and may experience great beauty in this form.

12. For more on this distinction between the Word in the rite and the Word in the readings and its bearing on music, see Hurd, "Making the Text More Efficacious: The Communion Rite and the Communion Song," *Today's Liturgy* 28, No. 24 (2006), 21–26 and the two-part essay, "Seamless Garment: From Liturgical to Ritual Music," *Today's Liturgy* 24, No. 2 (2002), 12–16 and No. 3 (2002), 16–21.

13. Bernadette Farrell, "Bread for the World" (Portland, OR: OCP, 1990).

14. Suzanne Toolan, "I Am the Bread of Life" (Chicago: GIA, 1966).

15. The Creed, though also a response to the word of God, is not strictly speaking a prayer but a statement of faith.

16. M. Basil Pennington, *Lectio Divina* (New York: Crossroad, 1998), 61. For other helpful introductions to *lectio divina* see Mary Margaret Funk, *Lectio Matters* (Collegeville, MN: Liturgical Press, 2013), Thelma Hall, *Too Deep for Words* (New York: Paulist Press, 1988), and Mariano Magrassi, *Praying the Bible*, trans. Edward Hagman (Collegeville, MN: Liturgical Press, 1998).

17. See John Navone, *Seeking God in Story* (Collegeville, MN: Liturgical Press, 1990) 84–100.

18. Bernadette Farrell, "Christ Be Our Light" (Portland, OR: OCP, 1993).

19. Suzanne Toolan, "Jesus Christ, Inner Light," (Portland, OR: OCP, 1996).

20. Greg Hayakawa, "I Am the Light of the World" (Portland, OR: OCP, 1978); Christopher Walker, "Out of Darkness" (Portland, OR: OCP, 1989); Marty Haugen, "Shepherd Me, O God" (Chicago: GIA, 1986).

21. Pennington, *Lectio Divina*, 87–90. Compassion and action as outcomes of communion correspond to the traditional notion of the "fruits" of the Eucharist.

3

The Songs We Sing
The Two Languages of Worship

Tony Barr

Several years ago, in the obscurity of an East Anglian pub, I was in deep conversation with Bill Tamblyn about the texts of Huub Oosterhuis and the music of Bernard Huijbers. I was struck by Bill's explanation of why Bernard's music was so popular. "It is so full of charm," he explained, "rather like the picture on the front of the chocolate box." In England around Christmastime, boxes of chocolate have pretty pictures on their covers, typically snow scenes. I argued that Bernard's music was popular because it was a true reflection of life, and that it appeared to reach deep into the soul.

Reflecting on that conversation, I know we were both right. Furthermore, I think we were talking about not only Oosterhuis–Huijbers hymnody but the music of worship in general. Where must one look to find the music that has the capacity to charm while at the same time reaching into the heart, mind, and soul of the assembly?

In life, we encounter two basic types of language, that of charm and that of formation. The former provides comfort, security, and stability, while the latter excites, stimulates, and draws us out. From earliest childhood we are wooed by comforting and consoling sounds. But would we have ever left the womb or the cradle had we not been coerced by the more demanding, insistent sounds of encouragement, to reach outward and beyond? The one language makes us feel good; the other makes us want to feel *more* as we develop a hunger for knowledge and a thirst for learning.

Toward One Liturgical Language

Liturgy, as life, requires these two basic patterns of language. In worship, there must be both charm and insemination. We are told not to fear because God is with us; yet we are also told to take up our cross daily and follow. Instinctively, we prefer the language of charm, which says "stay put" and makes us feel secure. Yet this disposes us to resist the opportunity to step out and meet different challenges. It sees the new as a threat, a destruction of these already established, comforting ways.

This situation is especially true in regard to new music and text. Songs that charm while offering little in the way of challenge attract immediate attention and gain instant popularity. Such songs, which offer no new insights nor mediate deeper levels of understanding, prove to be instant hits. They do not require thought; it is enough to feel good about them. "Inspirational" songs generate unqualified interest, while songs of a more inseminational character, which invite and unsettle, are easily dismissed as irrelevant or even bothersome.

Commercial liturgical publishers, by their very nature, display a greater interest in what sells than in what fosters idealism about liturgical formation. Although one may not exclude the other, the main duty of the publisher is to produce music that generates income. Experience has taught that it is much easier to soothe the assembly with pleasing songs than to introduce new music that stirs new depths of understanding through text and musical form. The music of charm is indeed music to the publisher's ear. But this holds our assemblies for ransom, preventing them from being evangelized and perhaps even locking them into eternal immaturity. Sadly, this language of charm does not bring human beings to fullness of growth. It can even stunt, retard, and impede growth.

Creating a New Language

The true educator is one who is able to blend charm and depth into a single language. This will inevitably lead to the creation of a new language of worship. This may be seen in the partnership between Bernard Huijbers and Huub Oosterhuis, who looked to liturgical theology for clues as to the true nature of the musical and textual roles of the assembly in worship. Text writers and composers should not only be able to identify the assembly's expectations regarding their songs of worship (what Bernard describes as the true liturgical folksong of the people), but should also be analysts of Scripture and liturgy, archaeologists seeking the origins and meaning of the various rites and accompanying texts that constitute the liturgy.

To do this successfully, questions must be asked. What is the purpose of the rite? What does it mean? How did it originate? How has it evolved throughout history? What are we to make of it, and how should we interpret it, today? An essential tool of the educator, such as the liturgical composer and text writer, is to be able to challenge presuppositions about who we are, why we are gathering, and what we are doing in our various rites or stages of worship. A quality essential in the composer or text writer is to be able to abandon all assumptions and formulas for success and to expose certain intrinsic truths related to the occasions and opportunities within worship.

Preparing music and text for the rite of gathering is an example. Before the author writes a comprehensive script about the coming together of the assembly or the composer crafts a cleverly constructed open-form chant, there are many questions to be asked. What *is* the rite of gathering? Or, more precisely, what *are* the various rites within the gathering? How does the assembly actually come together? Is there a difference between the *gathering* of the assembly and the rite of *entrance* of the presider and ministers? What is the role of the presider in the initial formation of the assembly?

What lies behind approaching and venerating the altar? What is the history of the opening greeting? Where did the penitential rites originate? How many distinct elements have been blended into our one penitential rite? What is the "Glory to God" in terms of biblical theology? In Luke, it is seen to be a song of the *anawim*, the poor who lived in expectation of the coming messiah. How should its literary structure, an acclamatory hymn of fragmentary verses, determine a musical setting for cantor and assembly? What is the history and meaning of the opening collect prayer?

The composer and text writer of the gathering song, for example, should therefore be able to identify the purpose of the gathering, who *we* are who have been called to worship, who *God* is who has called us, and what literary precedents are to be found in the Scriptures that express the reasons for gathering. In the psalter alone there is an abundance of gathering texts. Should we be content with singing "Holy God We Praise Thy Name" and similar examples born of a bygone spirituality, or should we be more concerned about songs that affirm the assembly in their quest for God—songs such as "Who are we, we who now gather here?" or "Who are you, whose name we bear?"

Likewise, the composer and text writer of any psalm setting should not be content with fitting texts into basic chants accompanied by simple assembly responses without first exploring the cultic origins of each psalm in Israel's history. Both must first examine that text as a piece of literature with an eye to its various literary forms. Is it a litany or ballad? Is it didactic, entreaty or lament, hymn, song of ascent, or call to gather? And then each should investigate the psalm as a piece of cultic drama. Is it a processional gathering, a lamentation with oracular consultation, a priestly exhortation, a call to repentance or conversion, a ballad of remembrance, or a hymn of thanksgiving?

To arrive at conclusions about these inductive or deductive expeditions will often involve speculation, but there is an abundance of wealth to guide us in our quest. In the psalter the evidence may be *inductive*—that is, internal to the text itself—revealing vestigial trace references to earlier cultic activity, now thinly veiled by subsequent redaction processes. For example,

Psalm 34, which originally consisted of two separate testimonies to God's personal intervention at a time of illness or distress, was later woven into a catechism for teaching about a compassionate God, and it was subsequently morphed into a direct call to gather for worship. Or evidence may be *deductive*—external to the psalm text—clearly or partially indicated throughout the Scriptures about worship patterns on high feasts and special occasions. A good example is Psalm 24, alluded to in 2 Samuel 6 as David led the ark triumphantly into the temple after yet another victory in battle. Understanding both literary form and cultic context are essential if text writer and composer are to avoid the easy way of falling back on enticement and charm.

The Liturgical Text Writer and Composer

The insights of post-Vatican II liturgical theology suggest to the text writer that worship embraces much more than simply adoring God. The traditional language of worship, which sings only of God's holiness and human unworthiness, is no longer adequate for the task. In liturgy we celebrate a covenant that focuses on ourselves as well as on God. Worship now addresses a deity closer to hand, no longer One who is out there, beyond the realm of our perceptions and experiences.

Songs that speak only of God and are entirely theocentric in nature disregard the human voice in covenant. Texts require a language that also expresses the anxieties, sufferings, weaknesses, and alienation of people, as well as our hopes, memories, and expectations. We look for a language that reflects human reality and avoids pious platitudes. But by the same token, worship should not be an egocentric exercise, dwelling on little else but the human condition and our indignation against injustice.

It is possible for the text writer to strike a balance between these two extremes, looking to the *history of salvation* for the memory of One who has become our hope and our future, the One who has called us, formed us into a people, and given us a name. This very story gives us the strength and the power to call on that very One to be present among us once again and to remain eternally faithful to us, consistent and constant to those promises made on our behalf.

Perhaps it is not enough to begin worship with a song that praises the all holy God, demanding that we bow and bend low because of our unworthiness to approach the Almighty. Perhaps it may be more appropriate to sing about ourselves and why we are coming together through texts that cause us to challenge our presuppositions about who we are and about who God is for us. Then our expectations will neither limit our potential for growth nor diminish our capacity for being surprised! Such is the burden on the text writer. It is no longer sufficient to write texts that either make us feel good as we praise God in sweet terms or put us down for being at times unworthy sinners and at others jolly pilgrims gathering to praise God's holy name while hoping to see justice done.

At the same time, the composer needs to know that a good, catchy tune or a lingering, seductive melody may not be the best way of involving people in worship. A good melody will encourage people to join in the singing, but is this necessarily active participation in worship? To sing during worship is not the same as singing worship itself. The composer needs to explore musical forms as well as musical shapes, finding those best suited not only to wooing the assembly but also to drawing the faithful into the song and engaging the entire congregation in the liturgical action. Participation means much more than merely joining in the song. To be creatively involved in worship, each member of the assembly must respond by drawing on the very depths of his or her own resourcefulness, the *mind* as well as the *heart*. The music of charm alone will not accomplish this.

The *litany form* is one example, where people are being led by a sung prayer leader who is well-versed in the ancient art of incantation. In it there is an immediate rapport between song leader and assembly through dialogue. This takes place in brief, uncomplicated phrases that are more storytelling than theologizing, using basic elementary melodies and urgent-yet-simple rhythms to embody visual images drawn from Scripture. The *open form song*, often built around an assembly refrain, takes its character and dynamic directly from the rite or the occasion in which it is being used rather than the text, which has likewise been inspired by the occasion. The so-called *folksong/ballad* (a closed-form song) has an important role to play in retelling the stories of a people. *Songs of praise* play an important role too, especially when the assembly is aware of the warning from the prophets that there can be no praise without seeing justice done. Songs of dialogue, songs that teach (e.g., the catechetical/alphabetical psalms), songs that affirm (baptismal confessional acclamations, etc.), songs that express purpose or intention (processional gathering songs, songs of approaching God's house and altar, songs that accompany the breaking and sharing of bread and wine), are all ways in which participants, text, music, and rite are integrated.

According to Huijbers, the functionality of liturgical music is to blend participant, text, and liturgical rite into one occasion. Some would say that the music *of* worship engages the assembly in a resourceful manner in the shaping of worship, while music *for* worship is no more than a device to get people joining in, regardless of the liturgical action going on at the same time. The power and creative energy of text writer and composer allows the assembly to become ministers of celebration.

A Responsive and Responsible Assembly

The purpose of music in worship is not to make people feel secure. On the contrary, liturgical text and music should "politicize the assembly," opening the individual and collective eye in a lengthy process of "conscientization" or awareness-building. This could well result in disturbing the faithful somewhat, as each individual becomes responsible for the development, well-being, and growth of the entire assembly and, ultimately, for the liberation of the whole world, driving out poverty, overcoming repression, and restoring peace, balance, and harmony everywhere. In the memorable words of Tom Conry and his predecessors, to make worship is to make revolution. Through the attitude formation that occurs whenever the assembly gathers to remember the word of God and give thanks, through the transformation that happens each time the assembly gathers to break bread and share the cup of blessing, each individual within the assembly is empowered to renew the face of the earth.

To pray "your kingdom come" is to assume the responsibility of making that happen. The assembly gathers to hear again the stories of the One-Who-Is-For-Us (one translation of YHWH), a God of Covenant, who said I-Shall-Be-There-For-You-If-You-Will-Be-My-People. When we hear these stories, we grow deeper in faith, wisdom, maturity, and discipleship. These stories not only charm us but ask something of us. In response, we give thanks, a creative activity that draws us away from ourselves. To adequately hear the word and to give thanks, the language of charm is insufficient. For the Good News to reach inside, the language of depth formation must accompany the language of charm.

The picture on the outside of the chocolate box is not enough to delight the human heart. The wrapping must be opened and the picture discarded to get to the chocolates. The charm of the picture, the sugar in the chocolate, soon leaves us feeling let down. Clearly, another language is needed to make us think and appreciate, going beyond appearances to further enhance our sensitivity and develop our sense of responsibility to the full. Huijbers always maintained that the only truly liturgical songs are those that mediate new levels of understanding each time we sing them.

Speaking in Human or Angelic Tongue

Charm—and insemination. These exist as the two poles of life and growth. Neither, however, should stand alone. A fully balanced person has responded to both. For worship to be truly human as well as wholly divine, both languages should be allowed an equal voice. Otherwise, we will never know the answer to that first question of why we have gathered here. And then we will never discover who we are or who God is.

Summary

This little reflection is intended to help in the responsible planning of worship each week. In looking for music that charms and seduces, we are cautioned that perhaps we should be looking for another important quality in our texts and songs, one that *invites* and *challenges* us to growth and a deeper understanding about our faith and ourselves.

Borrowing from liberation theology, then, one may say that if liturgy is to be effective, it must be tested in the lives of the worshiping assembly. The assembly that expects the music to be *uplifting* brings to the gathering the same limited expectations as it does to watching television. In contrast, the assembly that has gathered to be *energized* by its liturgy has heard the invitation to discipleship and wishes to respond. We do well to feel secure in the risen Christ, who is our hope and our future. But we must also reflect seriously on the command to be disciples, to leave the empty tomb behind us, abandoning all to follow a road that leads to death and beyond.

There is no clear-cut black and white here, but only varying shades of bright gray. The songs of worship must attract or they will not win the hearts of the assembly. But they must also reach the minds of the assembly, otherwise the assembly will never grow. The responsibility is on our composers and text writers to provide the right language for the assembly, a blend of both charm and insemination.

Out of Vatican II has evolved a theology of worship that sees the gathering as an occasion for renewing the covenant, providing the opportunity for the people and their God to meet once again in dialogue. We make this happen when we gather to hear the stories of our salvation told again and to break bread and share the blessing cup in thanksgiving for the God of Promise who is always present among us.

4

Moving to *Metamelos*
A New Heart, a New Church, a New Song

Rory Cooney

In titling this chapter "Moving to *Metamelos*," I'm deliberately coining a word that I hope will enable us to start thinking seriously about what puts the "new" in "sing a new song to the Lord." It's not that no one has thought of this before, but it's high time that together we reflect again upon the answers to an important question: *Who* is singing *what* song to *what* Lord? If that seems obvious to you, bear with me, because I think I have more questions to ask along the way.

First of all, *metamelos* is a simple construction that is parallel to the familiar word *metanoia*, a scriptural and theological word that means "a change of mind." More than this, however, *metanoia* has the sense of a revolution, a complete turning away from one direction and moving in another with all one's being and not just what we twenty-first-century children of the postenlightenment world call "the mind." *Metamelos*, then, means "a change of song," and I'm not completely sure what that will look like. Like the empire of God, which is the object of *metanoia*, or conversion, *metamelos* will be characterized by healing—perhaps that of rifts between musicians and styles and liturgical ideologies. It will be characterized by *shalom* and *agape*, rather than fear, jealousy, and triumphalism. It will sing about a God who is complete self-gift, who pours Self out, whose love is so utter that to our eyes and hearts trapped in time and enslaved to our desires it looks like death. In truth, it is the fullness of life, and it is what we call the paschal mystery.

My contention is that the church, instead of consistently and categorically worshiping the God of Jesus, has let its religious imagination about God be shaped by the empire that surrounds it. Rather than listening to the Word of the Savior and the apostles that has been its heart and treasure, letting its image of God and therefore its self-image be shaped by that Word, we in the church have for too long been distracted by—and have even coveted—the image of emperor and empire. We were offered the empire of God, and we settled, by and large, for the empire of Constantine and Charlemagne. This is apparent in nearly every aspect of church culture, but nowhere more obvious than in our music. What is needed now, more than ever, is repentance: a change of attitude, a complete turning, that will change the direction of our worship and the allegiance of our hearts. *Metanoia* will lead to *metamelos*. Without *metanoia*, we will continue to sing the song of empire, praising a God of power and might, while our unique *kerygma* is of a God whose nature is *kenosis* and *agape*.

In short, we've allowed our image of God to be shaped by empire, even though revelation requires that at some point we choose to do the opposite: shape our image of "empire" by who God is. But what does this mean? What kind of shift is required of us? This shift is the subject of the gospels and the whole New Testament. It is at the heart of the meaning of the incarnation. It is what Jesus was getting at when, on the way to Jerusalem, he told his disciples, "You know that those who are recognized as rulers over the Gentiles lord it over them, and their great ones make their authority over them felt. But it shall not be so among you. Rather, whoever wishes to be great among you will be your servant; whoever wishes to be first among you will be the slave of all" (Mark 10:42-44).

I want to expand this thought a little bit. As many scholars have demonstrated, the call of Jesus to "repent, believe the gospel, for the empire of God is at hand" is a call to turn away from one worldview to another.[1] In the "matrix" of the Roman Empire, with its own god (Caesar) and its version of peace and prosperity (the *Pax Romana*), the political and economic inequalities and burdens on its conquered subjects were abundantly clear, at least to the subjugated. As an alternative Jesus preached and lived "the empire of God," with its "jubilee economy" of peace through justice. Characterized by healing and exorcism that reconciled the alienated to family and community, and by a table-fellowship that shocked and angered those responsible for the interpretation of the socially organizing religious laws of Judaism, the kingdom-preaching of Jesus also used parables to allow disciples to reimagine a world different from the one they had come to accept as the only possible reality.

Key to this new imagining of reality is the deliberately chosen central imagining of God as *abba*. This choice is significant as much for what it leaves out (e.g., God as judge, king, or warrior) as for what it suggests. And while *abba* was not unheard of as divine nomenclature among first-century Jews, Jesus' use of the term seems to have included the insistence that *abba* was not just the father of Jews and their intimates, but of all people everywhere. This prophetic thread had been present in Jewish thought since the exile, but in Jesus and later in the preaching of the disciples, preeminently Paul and later Peter, it became a distinguishing and ultimately identifying characteristic. The idea that all people, and not just the Jews, were heirs to the covenantal promise was a major source of conflict in the gospels, more than once resulting in attempts on Jesus' life.

The organizing force of this universal "family" of the children of *abba* was not to be coercion or "lording it over" each other but service. Following the "way" of Jesus would mean choosing to serve: "whoever wishes to be great among you will be your servant; whoever wishes to be first among you will be the slave of all. For the Son of Man did not come to be served but to serve" (Mark 10:45). This behavior is clearly contrasted with the "empires of the world," because "those who are recognized as rulers over the Gentiles lord it over them, and their great ones make their authority over them felt. But it shall not be so among you" (Mark 10:42-43). The Gospel of Mark highlights the disciples missing this point, because Mark frames their jockeying for position in the Messiah's coming reign each time by words of Jesus emphasizing the cross and service.

We can take some consolation that we composers and pastoral musicians of the twenty-first century aren't the first to mishear the Good News.

Beyond these brief descriptions of the attributes of God's empire, there is the trajectory of the fourth gospel's movement of the *logos*. "In the beginning was the Word," says John. But "the word became flesh and dwelt among us." The *logos*, the Word, self-expression, the Identity of God, left behind the home of being "with God" and became a human being. At the Last Supper, the master kneels as a slave to wash the feet of the disciples with the instruction, "I have given you a model to follow, so that as I have done for you, you should also do" (John 13:15). Thus the very path of God is traced from the unknown Beyond to the feet of the disciples. At the end, with Jesus' last breath, John says, "he handed over the spirit" (19:30), at once completing the act of the self-emptying *logos* begun at the incarnation and pouring out the life of God into the world forever through the ministry of the church.

This next corner is the hardest to turn, but it seems to me it is as important as anything we believe. Jesus Christ is the image of the invisible God, says the letter to the Colossians. In John's gospel Jesus tells Philip, who has asked Jesus to show them the Father: "Whoever has seen me has seen the Father" (John 14:9). Matthew too acknowledges this identification of Jesus with the Father: "Whoever receives me receives the one who sent me" (Matt 10:40). If Christ is the image of the invisible God, if Jesus the human being reveals the Father to us, revealing an empire "not like those of this world," then why do we image God like a warrior ("Lord") and an all-powerful King, rather than as one who dwells among us, showing us the path to life that is nonviolent, justice-seeking, healing, equality-building, and self-emptying?

I'll never forget the first North American Academy of Liturgy meeting I attended in 1991, the year that David Power, OMI, was given the Berakah award. In his response he articulated a shattering truth that helped me begin to understand how we went wrong. His point was that when a Christian confesses that "Jesus Christ is Lord," as Paul proclaims at the end of the famous "kenosis hymn" of Philippians, we do not mean that Jesus Christ is the Lord like the lords we know from this world. We mean that lordship is redefined by who Jesus is—that is, servant, healer, breadbreaker, speaker of truth to power, gatherer, and (sometimes) iconoclast. For the first time in my life, I realized how true it is that Constantine did the church no favors by making Christianity the religion of the empire. Since that time, I've applied a hermeneutic of suspicion to all interaction between church and state, which means that I spent ten very suspicious years in the United States following the 2000 election.

We have fallen, by and large, into the same linguistic trap as the apostles. Hearing that the "kingdom of God is at hand," we immediately stopped listening, focusing our imagination on how it will be when we win, the other guys lose, and we're in the kingdom of Jesus. Like the apostles before us, we imagine a messianic general who will slay the evildoers and make us the winners. Therefore our imagination has become lodged there, and we've not been able to reimagine a world where, in Bob Hurd's happy phrase, *"poder es servir, porque Dios es amor"* (power is in serving, because God is love).[2] There, kingdom is not defined by its ability to coerce or wallow in luxury, but in how well its subjects imitate its "king" in washing feet, healing, peacefully speaking the truth to power, and reconciling those on the margins of life.

As a choir boy in grammar school and then in seminary high school, the repertoire of my worship was organ, *a cappella* music (mostly chant, accompanied or not), and music from early post-Vatican II Catholic hymnals, a lot of which came from Reformation-era hymnists. I can remember thrilling to singing words like these by Robert Grant, and I suspect that they continue to thrill worshipers in English-speaking countries:

> O worship the King all glorious above!
> O gratefully sing his power and his love,
> Our shield and defender, the Ancient of Days,
> Pavilioned in splendor and girded with praise.
>
> O tell of his might, O sing of his grace,
> Whose robe is the light, whose canopy, space;
> Whose chariots of wrath the deep thunderclouds form,
> And dark is his path on the wings of the storm.[3]

Like many hymns and songs ancient and modern, "O Worship the King" is studded with the vocabulary and imagery of monarchy and power. This is to be expected. Empire and kingdom have been the lenses through which humanity has viewed the divine for millennia, including that sliver of humanity known as Judaism, nestled on the roads where empires of the Mediterranean to the west and those of the Tigris and Euphrates to the east perennially collided. Kings and emperors were not simply the chosen of the gods; they were, often enough, gods themselves. As the organizing force of civilization, empires took on divine attributes, and coopted or transmogrified religion in such a way as to validate their claim to divine authority. Nor are the economic and political empires of today immune from this idolatry.

Brian Wren's 1989 book, *What Language Shall I Borrow? God-Talk in Worship*, included a whimsical chapter in which an alien civilization studies the Christian view of God by looking through the 1983 Methodist hymnal of England.[4] The report distills the 328 songs about "God's nature" for their language. Of the 328 hymns, "the most frequent metaphor is of God as a dominant male, a king who rules and gives commands."[5] Wren uses the acronym *KINGAFAP* to describe these images:

King-God-Almighty-Father-Protector. He claims that 190 of the hymns in this section of the hymnal, or about 60 percent, employ this dominant imagery. I suspect that, whoever we are and wherever we sing, we recognize this kind of language in our worship, both in the songs we sing and prayers we pray. It's not simply the language of monarchy to which I am calling attention, but the language of power, even benevolent power.

Across the pond in 2006, the National Association of Pastoral Musicians (NPM) conducted a survey of the music in American parishes called "Songs that Make a Difference," which attempted to discover which pieces of music in the American repertoire (mostly Catholic, but not exclusively so) "made a lasting impact" on people's faith lives by actually asking people to name a song and talk about it.[6] NPM received 3,000 responses to the survey, naming 670 different songs. The highest-rated song, "On Eagle's Wings," was the choice of only eight percent (about 240) of respondents. Looking at the top 25 songs, a much broader range of divine imagery is immediately visible, including two with the word "servant" in the title, though the texts make no explicit claims about the deity.

I bring this up not to compare the two at all; they are British apples and California oranges. However, the data does demonstrate two things that I think we all know in our bones. First, the imagery of empire, of power and might, riches and victory, dominate much of our God-talk in Christian worship, and it's not just in the music we have continued to hold out of tradition and respect. Contemporary music, too—and I must especially point to much of the "praise" music that finds its way into Catholic worship in the United States, conjures an "awesome God" who is awesome by virtue of violence and force against enemies and ruling over a celestial palace that is beyond our words, though not beyond our attempts to describe its gilded and bejeweled splendor.

Second, turning our attention to the American survey, we see a predictably democratic excising of some of the images of monarchy and power in favor of other images: gathering, intimacy, shepherd, servant, bread, eagle, city, and beatitude. This is all the more remarkable when we consider that hymnals themselves still hold a large number of Wren's *KINGAFAP* musical texts. But the issue with the American list is this: where is the music that inspires works of mercy? Where is the music that cries "Kyrie eleison" for violence shown to others, for the exploitation of the environment, for the poverty and despair engendered by corporate greed and exploitation of people? At its best, the list might be seen as a catalog of songs to comfort the comfortable, and at its worst, as the opium that dulls the sense of urgency toward advocating for the empire of God in the face and in the midst of the greatest economic empire that has ever populated the planet. American liturgical music risks being the lullaby that enables the church to sleep through the machinations of empire and focus its eyes inward in a petty individualism while the world burns around it.

Why is all this important? In 2007 the United States Conference of Catholic Bishops issued a document, *Sing to the Lord*, that acknowledges that musicians are "first of all disciples. . . . Like other baptized members of the assembly, pastoral musicians need to hear the Gospel, experience conversion, profess faith in Christ, and so proclaim the praise of God" (49). We ourselves are called to *metanoia*, a change of heart, to hear the good news of divine love that is showered equally upon all, and to turn away from the empire of force and acquisition toward the empire of *agape* and *kenosis*. But until we are broken of our habits of hearing this message written too small, written about "me and Jesus" and not about losing ourselves to find ourselves in the community of the world, we have not really moved from *eros* to *agape*.

So we return to the question I asked at the outset: What song needs to be sung? To what Lord? And what makes it *new*? Though our songs—like our imagination and our whole lives—may have been tainted by the idolatry of empire and praised a status quo wrought by a Caesar posing as God, they don't have to stay that way. The *metanoia* of church musicians will surely reinvigorate our repertoire, and the result will be *metamelos*, a new song of praise that will mirror the truth of the foot-washing *logos*, the God who did not imagine that divinity was something to be hoarded, but who poured himself out, becoming a slave to us *when we were sinners*, believers in the truth of empire and not of *agape*.

Walter Brueggemann's *Israel's Praise*, a foundational work for pastoral musicians, offers the pattern of doxology in the psalter as a way of weighing the validity of worship in every time and place, especially our own. Memory, lament, and thanksgiving will keep our praise honest:

> Out of such singing against idols . . . Israel will sing with abandonment, without restraint. Israel will sing because it has this odd One before whom to sing. Israel will sing because it has this inexplicable passion against suffering and it has learned that silence breeds suffering. . . . Doxology, even well intentioned, falls prey to and is co-opted by ideology and idolatry. But . . . it does not follow that doxology inevitably becomes idolatry and ideology. . . . In the end, after the long season of suspicion, we hear Israel's faithful voice in song and doxology.[7]

Music can indeed "sing a new church" into being. In fact, our singing will "sing a new God into reality" in this world by singing "different hymns than the conventions of royal reality."[8] Turning away from the sin of living in the kingdom of Constantine and believing (that is, loving with our whole heart and life) in the good news of the empire of God and in Jesus Christ, the icon of *that* reality will be the catalyst of the new song sung by a new people. It will be a song of the Way, the cross, and *agape*. Its music will part the sea, and break down the walls of Jericho. No sword will be drawn, and not a shot will be fired. This great doxology, sung in time and space by disciples, is the sound of Christ singing in the Holy Spirit. It is Christ, head and members, emptying Self in the one song of *kenosis* and *agape* to the self-emptying Abba. God, who makes all things new, will, in us, sing a new church, a new world, into being.

Notes

1. See, for instance, John Dominic Crossan, *God and Empire: Jesus against Rome, Then and Now* (San Francisco: Harper San Francisco, 2007) and Marcus Borg and John Dominic Crossan, *The Last Week: What the Gospels Really Teach About Jesus's Final Days in Jerusalem* (San Francisco: Harper San Francisco, 2006).

2. Bob Hurd and Pia Moriarty, From "Pan de Vida," by Bob Hurd and Pia Moriarty. © 1988, Bob Hurd and Pia Moriarty (Portland, OR: OCP, 1988).

3. Robert Grant, "O Worship the King" (1833).

4. Brian Wren, *What Language Shall I Borrow? God-Talk in Worship: A Male Response to Feminist Theology* (New York: Crossroad, 1989), 116ff.

5. Ibid., 119.

6. "Songs that Make a Difference," http://www.npm.org/assets/Songs-Difference.pdf

7. Walter Brueggemann, *Israel's Praise: Doxology against Idolatry and Ideology* (Philadelphia: Fortress, 1998), 152–53.

8. Ibid., 153.

5

Beauty and Suitability in Music in the Liturgy

Paul Inwood

When faced with any particular musical "action" that takes place in liturgy, is it possible to make a judgment on the intrinsic value of that action? Can we say that a particular piece is more or less good? My thesis is that the answer is *yes*, but that the criteria on which we base such a judgment require further examination. For the trained musician, the musical worth of a piece can be ascertained according to "classical" criteria. The liturgist will have a different viewpoint, however, evaluating the piece on how it functions in the rite. The "consumer" may well be coming from a different place again: Does it lift me up in prayer? To decide whether musical or aesthetic or liturgical principles should be paramount is to evade the possibility that a combination of all of these is possible and indeed essential.

Concepts of Music in the Church

In order to explore this properly, it will be helpful to review briefly the various concepts of music—both within and outside the church—that have been current over the centuries and the differences between those concepts. Broadly speaking, people have talked about

- religious music,
- sacred music,
- church music,
- liturgical music,
- and ritual music.[1]

How do we define each of these, and how do we differentiate between them?

Religious music

The Wikipedia entry for this term immediately confuses things by including sacred music, Christian music, church music, and gospel music under this same category, rather than differentiating between them. The basic definition runs: "Religious music (also sacred music) is music performed or composed for religious use or through religious influence." This definition is not entirely satisfactory—it would be more correct to say that religious music is music that is religious in flavor and uses religious imagery or even religious texts (e.g., poetry). In other words, religious music is the broadest possible definition of a general relationship between music and organized religion. It does not matter which religion is in question. Some would say that it does not matter if no particular religion is involved at all; it is the generally religious flavor that counts.

The commentary on the first Universa Laus document says: "'Religious music' remains rather vague, and indicates any music born of a religious sentiment or composed from the starting-point of a religiously-inspired text."[2]

Sacred music

The classic text on this topic is Pius X's motu proprio from 1903, *Tra le Sollecitudini*. Defining the characteristics of sacred music, the document says that sacred music should possess "sanctity and goodness of form, which will spontaneously produce the final quality of universality. It must be holy, and must, therefore, exclude all profanity not only in itself, but in the manner in which it is presented by those who execute it. It must be true art, for otherwise it will be impossible for it to exercise on the minds of those who listen to it that efficacy which the Church aims at obtaining in admitting into her liturgy the art of musical sounds."[3]

It will be seen that this definition is as generic as that for religious music. The commentary on the first Universa Laus document says: "'Sacred music' is equally a general notion in the same sort of line as ['religious music' and 'church music'], but here we can see that the aim is to establish a clear boundary with 'profane' music."[4]

The term "sacred music" originated in a document by (Lutheran) Michael Praetorius in 1614, and it did not become part of the Catholic Church's vocabulary until the end of the eighteenth century, when it served to underpin a desire for "purity" and a generally conservative agenda. It is normally used in a very limited geographical sense, and it takes no account of the fact that the notion of the sacred belongs to the whole of humanity (even pagans) and is not limited to Christianity.

Church music

Most people would understand this to mean music that is intended to be sung or played in a church building. It can include what we may loosely term "spiritual concert music," such as cantatas, oratorios, or even Benjamin Britten's "church operas"—works designed to be performed in a church setting and yet not part of the liturgy as such.

The commentary on the first Universa Laus document says: "'Church music' is close to 'religious music' but, by specifying the place where this music is normally performed, the term includes connotations of volume of space and atmosphere (fullness, solemnity, etc.)."[5]

Liturgical music

Here we are talking about music that is designed for use within a liturgy, but not yet about a tight relationship between the elements of the rite and the music used.

The commentary on the first Universa Laus document says: "'Liturgical music' turns our minds towards the use of music in the course of a celebration, and emphasizes the functional link between musical art and liturgy, at the same time distancing itself from an exclusively aesthetic conception of music."[6]

We could say that a great deal of music is designed to be used in a liturgical context, but it may not necessarily grow out of the liturgy as an integral part of it. It may indeed be imposed on the liturgy or inserted into it without due regard for what the rite is trying to do.

Ritual music

The description in the commentary on the first Universa Laus document cannot be improved: "'Ritual music' translates and underlines the deep union that we are seeking between a particular kind of music and the rite for which it has been composed, or selected, or performed."[7]

This term speaks of the close link between music and the rite, which, as indicated above, may sometimes be lacking. It says nothing about how beautiful or otherwise it may be. The term was appropriated by the Milwaukee Statement in 1992.[8]

What is suitable or appropriate?

John Paul II's approach to this question is classic. He asks for holiness, prayer, dignity, beauty, soundness of form, full adherence to the liturgical text, synchronization with the liturgy, and bringing out the nature proper to a specific rite.[9]

Saint Augustine takes a rather different approach. His original treatise on the subject is lost, but fortunately he refers to it in his *Confessions* where he speaks of two different aspects of a thing: its beauty, and the way in which it harmonizes with something else.[10] For Augustine, it is not sufficient that a shoe be beautiful (*pulchrum*); it must also fit properly (*aptum*).

This brilliant insight makes it clear that our notions of what is beautiful must be broadened considerably. We cannot just define something as being in a particular category (as outlined above) with whatever qualities we attribute to that category. John Paul II's desire for synchronization with the liturgy comes closest to Augustine's *aptum* criterion.

Can we define beauty in music?

The authors of the Snowbird Statement (1995) spoke passionately about the need for beauty in music for the liturgy, and yet they were unable to produce a definition or provide any criteria by which it could be judged except by negative comparisons. Thus the beauty of God's self-revelation is contrasted with the pragmatic, ideological, or political ends of some forms of liturgy.[11] Snowbird rightly affirms standards of excellence in composition and performance, but claims that much contemporary ritual music is hampered by excessive academicism, artless rationality, or utilitarian functionalism.[12] In the end they are forced back on the self-evident statement that some music is better than other music and that "there are those who, through training and talent, are able to identify music that is technically, aesthetically and expressively good."[13] Cynics have suggested that this is tantamount to saying "Yes, beauty exists, and we are the ones who are going to tell you what it is!"

Other authors have attempted the definition, too. At one end of the spectrum the philosopher William James essentially defined beauty as the element or quality that we can find nowhere else. This is another definition by means of a negative, though he does refer to the religious feel of beautiful music. At the other end sits Orlando Fedeli, for whom it's all about proportions, number, and dimensions. For Fedeli, the actual relationship of the sound frequencies produces the sensation of beauty, and he adduces the same argument for beauty in architecture.[14] In this respect he is a disciple of Augustine, for whom numbers and proportions were also important.[15]

Augustine also looks at the difference between love and lust, and he attempts to define the difference between physical attraction and metaphysical attraction. In the course of this he seems to be saying that attraction may be triggered not only by the pleasant qualities of an object but also by a desire for knowledge. In being drawn toward something, we long to know more about it; and in acquiring that knowledge we may well have an appreciation of it that goes beyond its mere attractiveness. Indeed, he cites an example whereby one may be attracted out of natural curiosity to something that is in fact quite ugly.[16]

May that which makes one shudder be considered beautiful? Is there a terrible beauty inherent in something of which one is even mortally afraid? In terms of music or architecture, can the stark, the austere, the bare, the clashing dissonance, the unpleasant tone-quality still be considered to be in some way *beautiful*? Can beauty, in fact, be ugly? This is surely the paradox of the cross.

In a postmodern world, the whole notion of beauty has reached a point where the two statements "It made me feel really good! It's beautiful" and "It made me feel really bad! It's beautiful" are equally legitimate and equally true. Modern civilization has desensitized people to the point where any extreme experience may be interpreted as giving pleasure. Perhaps this phenomenon is following the line of William James again: being radically different confers value on an artistic experience.

Another element in the discussion is tedium. Musicians, like the authors of the Snowbird Statement, have often confused idiom with quality. And yet we know that there is good and bad in all idioms and that value cannot be defined by musical style. In the same way that there is both good and bad contemporary music in the liturgy, we must be honest and admit that in our libraries there are rooms full of substandard sixteenth-century polyphony and acres of frankly mediocre Gregorian chant.

And one of the distinguishing characteristics of such music is that it is very boring, unlike the music of static composers such as Arvo Pärt, John Tavener, or in other domains Steve Reich or Philip Glass. Those artists know how to craft the contemplative dimension of music so that it is constantly but subtly changing and developing. In a different realm, Jacques Berthier's Taizé music did the same.[17]

There is a difference between the kind of repetition that promotes meditation and contemplation and the kind of repetition that is simply monotonous. The answer to this conundrum may lie in the composer's craft and experience combined with the inspiration of the Holy Spirit. One cannot do without the other—both are necessary.

In the final analysis, it is often quite difficult for people to agree on what is beautiful and what is not. It seems to come down to "Beauty is in the eye of the beholder" once more—*de gustibus non disputandum,* or "there's no accounting for taste!"

Can we define suitability in music?

Here we are on much firmer ground. *Sacrosanctum Concilium*'s statement that "sacred music is to be considered the more holy in proportion as it is more closely connected with the liturgical action" (112) was groundbreaking, even shocking, in its time.

This is the first modern manifestation in a church document of Augustine's principle of *aptum,* as opposed to the emphasis of previous documents on the *pulchrum*. This is not to say that *Sacrosanctum Concilium* does not include the aesthetic in its definition—indeed it does when it refers in the same paragraph to music adding delight to prayer, fostering unity of minds, or conferring greater solemnity upon the sacred rites. But these functions are secondary to the close connection with the liturgical action. Though the council fathers did not put it this way, the best music is that which fits the ritual "like a glove."

This was the inspiration for the celebrated threefold judgment—liturgical, pastoral, and musical—proposed in paragraph 25 of *Music in Catholic Worship* and unpacked in greater detail in paragraphs 26–41.[18] This threefold judgment has enjoyed a broad influence in the years since it first appeared in 1972.[19] Although neither MCW nor its supplementary successor *Liturgical Music Today* specifically dealt with the question of beauty, they are clear about the need for a combined and balanced way of evaluating the suitability of music for use in liturgy.[20]

These insights were taken a stage further in the Milwaukee Statement, which among other things treats music as a language of faith and emphasizes the symbolic power of music. Important sections follow the pathway forged by *Sacrosanctum Concilium* 112 with in-depth discussions of liturgical and musical structures, textual and lyrical considerations, and cross-cultural music-making.[21] Without a doubt, however, the section of this document that drew the most attention was its evaluation and development of the threefold judgment. It criticized a tendency to make three separate judgments rather than a single combined judgment, and it called for an integrated judgment incorporating all three dimensions.[22] Furthermore, it stated that the most crucial context in making this judgment was the cultural context.[23] For example, what is right in a Vietnamese context will not necessarily be so in a Hispanic context, and vice versa.

Here was an approach to making an informed judgment as to the appropriateness of every piece of music to be used in liturgy, a judgment that would blend the different gifts and insights of those representing the various strands. In many places this has still to be achieved. It must be admitted that this is partly due to the fact that the cultural judgment, perhaps alongside a pastoral one, has pride of place, with the liturgical and musical components lagging far behind.

It would be possible to add yet another judgment to the mix, one that does not receive very much attention. This would be a *theological* or *textual* judgment. Here we are not only in the realm of potential heresy (a small number of frequently-used pieces do in fact "make statements about faith that are untrue"[24]), but we encounter a more widespread problem in which average-to-bad texts are being carried by good music. The music setting ends up disguising the shortcomings of the text; "ghastly words carried by a good tune" is one common expression for this. It can often happen with some of the more personalist utterances of contemporary Christian artists. There will be more to say about this in the following section, but here let us simply say that in the case of lyrics that are not actual texts of the liturgy it will be important to include an objective evaluation of the text as well as the music.

An almost unnoticed part of the Milwaukee Statement was paragraph 85, which stated that any integrated evaluation of music in worship must take into account the *performance* of the music and not simply evaluate the music in its printed form.[25] It referred in particular to incorporating an evaluation of *the quality of the musicians* into the mix.[26]

This is a delicate area to tackle. One question to ask is: Are these the most appropriate musicians to be performing this particular kind of music, or these particular pieces? Their suitability (of lack thereof) can be just as crucial to the rite as is the question of whether the music theoretically "fits" the liturgy or not. The Milwaukee Statement wisely draws attention to the improvisatory nature of some liturgical music—for example, gospel music or the music of Taizé.[27] To this one could add organ "noodling" and impromptu harmonizations or descants for final verses of hymns—to name but two additional examples. We need to acknowledge that while some musicians are highly gifted improvisers, others with the best intentions will quite simply never be able to manage it. Similarly, even in music that does not require these improvisatory skills, some musicians will make a good job of some styles of music while totally failing to get inside other styles. How do we put in place a mechanism for discerning people's gifts and utilizing them, rather than assuming that everyone is potentially capable of doing everything?

Another related observation concerns the role of trained musicians in liturgy. Sometimes one encounters trained musicians who look down their noses at particular styles or idioms and refuse to take part in them. They have not realized how much their technical skills and experience can contribute to music that they may even despise, transforming it into something at a completely different and wonderful level. Incidentally, this form of prejudice is by no means limited to "classical" musicians; just as many "folk" musicians denigrate choir/organ music as old-fashioned, fuddy-duddy, and boring as the classical musicians who despise folk or Hispanic music as primitive and unformed. Collaborative working is what we should be striving for. The results can be unexpectedly good!

Can we synthesize beauty and suitability?

Here we enter what may be called the "spiritual" dimension, where music is suited not only to the liturgy and the ambient culture but also to the business of lifting hearts and minds to God. As *Sing to the Lord* puts it, "The *spiritual dimension* of sacred music refers to its inner qualities that enable it to add greater depth to prayer, unity to the assembly, or dignity to the ritual. Sacred music is holy when it mediates the holiness of God and forms the Holy People of God more fully into communion with him and with each other in Christ."[28]

What I am proposing is that the combination of beauty and suitability is best achieved *in a context of prayer*. Not only are selections appropriate when judged by all the dimensions mentioned above, but the music is additionally a means to genuine prayer. People's spiritual lives are nourished by it; it provides a foundation for growth and development.

This is a somewhat intangible area to grasp, and it would be necessary to say immediately that there is a danger of relapsing into sentimentality—which, of course, not all musicians and assemblies manage to resist. Often this can be the result of texts that are overbalanced toward the emotional sphere. The answer is not to revert to texts that are overly cerebral, but to find a middle way. It is also worth reminding ourselves that the liturgy is a public, communal activity, as contrasted with individual private prayer, hence the oft-repeated dictum that texts used in liturgy should tend toward using the first-person plural rather than the first-person singular. A look at the psalter reveals an excellent balance between both "I" and "We" psalms, as well as those written in the third-person singular and plural.

Sentimentality can also be present in the music. The sliding chromaticisms of mawkish Victorian drawing-room ballads have found their way into some music that is used in liturgy, for example. When combined with texts that are too heavily charged with emotion, the results can be extreme. But other manifestations of musical sentimentality may also be found—in the music of some ethnic communities and in the music of contemporary Christian artists, LifeTeen composers, and others. Here is a real source of tension for multicultural and mixed communities.

Sing to the Lord reminds us that "Music does what words alone cannot do. It is capable of expressing a dimension of meaning and feeling that words alone cannot convey. While this dimension of an individual musical composition is often difficult to describe, its affective power should be carefully considered along with its textual component."[29]

The question has been asked why devotionalism so often appears to go hand-in-hand with bad taste. It is not easy to respond to this, but the answer lies, once again, in redressing an overbalance toward the heart at the expense of the head. The best texts and music will achieve a good balance of both. Without this, I believe, communities will continue to be disunited, with the consequent risk that different groups of people may deride the spirituality of others. By taking a middle road, the repertoire will be "slightly detached," not belonging to any one group. In this way everyone must make some sacrifice for the good of the entire community, and it is to be hoped that they will embrace this sacrifice gladly.

When we have reached a stage where all groups can say openly and honestly to each other "I'm sorry, I just can't sing that. It turns me off," and where the groups then decide to do something that does not come completely naturally to any of them for the good of the whole, there is a chance for mutual growth and support.

This may not fulfill the demands of those for whom beauty is primarily to do with aesthetics, but if beauty can be seen in the fact of entire communities praying, praising, being fed, and growing together, then the developing integration of communities will be nothing but the most wonderful, most beautiful, and most appropriate achievement that liturgical musicians can help to accomplish.

Notes

1. Universa Laus, *Music in Christian Celebration*, 1.3:
   The vocal and instrumental practices integral to Christian liturgies can be called by many names. Common expressions such as "sacred music", "religious music" or "church music" have broad and rather nebulous meanings which do not necessarily relate to the liturgy at all. Even the expression "liturgical music" (in the United States "musical liturgy") may not be precise enough to denote the unique relationship between liturgy and music that we are talking about here. Throughout the remainder of this document, therefore, we shall use the expression "(Christian) ritual music".

2. Claude Duchesneau and Michel Veuthey, *Music and Liturgy: the Universa Laus Document and Commentary*, trans. Paul Inwood (Portland, OR: Pastoral Press, 1992), 38.

3. Pope Pius X, *Tra le Sollecitudini: Instruction on Sacred Music* (motu proprio, November 22, 1903), 2.

4. Duchesneau and Veuthey, *Music and Liturgy*, 38.

5. Ibid.

6. Ibid.

7. Ibid.

8. The Milwaukee Symposia for Church Composers: A Ten-Year Report, July 9, 1992, 6–7.

9. Pope John Paul II, Chirograph for the Centenary of the Motu Proprio "Tra le Sollecitudini" on Sacred Music, 4–6.

10. Augustine recalls his earlier *De pulchro et apto* (On the aesthetic of beauty and the fitting) in *Confessions* 4.13.20.

11. The Madeleine Institute, The Snowbird Statement on Catholic Liturgical Music (November 1, 1995), 3.

12. Ibid., 4, 5.

13. Ibid., 6.

14. Orlando Fedeli, "Beauty in Music," Montfort Cultural Association, section iv.

15. "When reason goes through heaven and earth, it discovers that nothing pleases it except beauty; and in beauty, the figures; in the figures the dimensions; in the dimensions, the numbers" (Augustine, *De Ordine* 2.15.42). "Can we love anything else but beauty? But it is harmony that pleases in beauty; well, as we already saw, harmony is the result of equality of proportions. This equal proportion is not just found in the manifestations of beauty proper to the realm of the ear or in those which result from the movement of bodies, but it exists yet in these visible forms, to which we usually give the name of beauty" (*De Musica* 6.13.38).

16. *Confessions* 2.5 and 10.35.

17. It is interesting to note that the Brothers at Taizé who have taken up Jacques Berthier's mantle have imitated the idiom but without the compositional craft to go with it. Elementary rules of harmony—which Berthier had within his bones—are ignored, or perhaps the Brothers are simply unaware of them, being self-taught. The result is music that sounds similar at a superficial level but may be torture for a trained musician.

This kind of phenomenon—the untrained or self-taught musician—continues to be at the root of much controversy today, when any composer can write choir harmonies or keyboard accompaniments and blithely breach every known academic rule, and who, when challenged, will say that he simply doesn't care, even going so far as to mock those who were brought up in the composer's craft.

The underlying question seems to be this: does beauty depend on keeping the rules? Or, on knowing the rules but choosing when to break them, using technique to produce a good result nevertheless? Today, the majority of composers will admit that *in terms of sound* some of the old precepts made a lot of sense. But they nevertheless continue not to learn them or observe them! There does not seem to be any prospect of an early resolution to this ongoing debate.

18. Bishops' Committee on the Liturgy, *Music in Catholic Worship* (Washington, DC: National Conference of Catholic Bishops, 1972 [rev. ed, 1983]).

19. Actually the threefold judgment first appeared in MCW's precursor, the little-known *The Place of Music in Eucharistic Celebrations* (Washington, DC: National Conference of Catholic Bishops, 1967).

20. Bishops' Committee on the Liturgy, *Liturgical Music Today: A Statement of the Bishops' Committee on the Liturgy on the Occasion of the Tenth Anniversary of Music in Catholic Worship* (Washington, DC: National Conference of Catholic Bishops, 1982). In fact, neither document ever mentions the word "beauty."

21. Milwaukee Statement, 37–44, 45–55, 56–63.

22. Ibid., 81–85, a recommendation continued in *Sing to the Lord*, 126–36.

23. Ibid., 86.

24. Sing to the Lord, 83.

25. This topic forms the kernel of my other essay in the present series of books: "How Music in the Liturgy is Perceived and Received: an Anthropological/Semiological Perspective," *The Heart of Our Music*, vol. 3, *Digging Deeper*, ed. John Foley (Collegeville, MN: Liturgical Press, 2015).

26. Milwaukee Statement, 85.

27. Ibid., 85.

28. *Sing to the Lord*, 69.

29. Ibid., 124.

6

From "God, Beyond All Names" to "O Agape"
Images of God in Liturgical Music

Jan Michael Joncas

I cannot think of a better contemporary liturgical hymn to introduce the issues raised by the images of God conveyed in our worship music than Bernadette Farrell's "God, Beyond All Names":

> God, beyond our dreams, you have stirred in us a memory;
> You have placed your powerful spirit in the hearts of humankind.
>
> *Refrain:* All around us we have known you, all creation lives to hold you.
> In our living and our dying we are bringing you to birth.
>
> God, beyond all names, you have made us in your image;
> We are like you, we reflect you; we are woman, we are man.
>
> God, beyond all words, all creation tells your story;
> You have shaken with our laughter, you have trembled with our tears.
>
> God, beyond all time, you are laboring within us;
> We are moving, we are changing, in your spirit ever new.

> God of tender care, you have cradled us in goodness,
> You have mothered us in wholeness, you have loved
> us into birth.[1]

Four of the five stanzas pursue the *via negativa*, declaring that God escapes all human language and conceptuality yet is powerful and active in human history. The final stanza embraces the *via positiva*, boldly applying a series of images to God that could arise from either human gender ("tender care," "cradled us," "loved us into birth") but cluster around a decidedly feminine image ("mothered us"), an image that had been prepared for us through the marvelous pun in verse four ("laboring within us"). If it is true—as the second stanza and Genesis 1:27 both tell us—that human beings differentiated by gender are the "image of God," then feminine images of God in addition to masculine images are conceivable. While none of the images in "God, Beyond All Names" would be shocking for readers of the *Odes of Solomon* or Julian of Norwich, they are decidedly different from the standard hymnic images of God as "mighty fortress," "creator of the earth and skies," "our help in ages past," "king," and "eternal Father." This is also not a standard hymnic exploration of the Divine Persons in relation to each other and to us. There is a reference to God's "powerful spirit" in the first verse, but given the lack of capitalization that spirit is not personalized as one of the Blessed Trinity. The third stanza declares that God has "shaken with our laughter" and "trembled with our tears," which presumably refers to the incarnation of the Second Person of the Blessed Trinity as the means by which God is able to do so, but neither the name of Jesus Christ nor any of his titles are explicitly evoked. Perhaps most dangerously the refrain asserts that "in our living and our dying we are bringing you to birth," a declaration that, while defensible at the level of mystic spirituality (as in Meister Eckhart), seems to run counter to a dogmatic understanding of the Triune God as eternal.

In this essay I would like to explore two types of divine imagery in liturgical music. An immediate difficulty is that the term "image" has as its primary referent something engaging the sense of sight and that is not my use of the term here. I extend the term's reference to two other categories: sonic/musical images—that is, acoustic events operating as signs or symbols of the transcendent within an *acoustic* meaning system; and verbal/textual images—that is, linguistic events operating as signs or symbols of the transcendent within a *linguistic* meaning system.

Sonic/Musical Images

I once had the privilege of attending Sunday Mass at St. Gervais in Paris where the Monastic Communities of Jerusalem, a post-Vatican II group dedicated to living a new form of monastic life in the heart of the city, regularly worship. A reader proclaimed the first reading in French, followed by a significant period of silence. The responsorial psalm's antiphon was intoned by a cantor and immediately repeated by the congregation, but with the monastic communities supporting the assembly's singing with four-part *a cappella* harmonies; the verses were sung by the cantor to a psalm-tone formula with the antiphon recurring after each. Again a significant period of silence descended. I was prepared to hear the second reading proclaimed when the organ began to play: a three-part improvisation that probably lasted eight minutes. I was taken aback until I realized the liturgical genius of this contemplative community. The first reading had recounted the visit of the three mysterious visitors to Abraham in Genesis 18, which some Christian traditions have seen as a foreshadowing of the revelation of God as triune. The organ improvisation was a sonic evocation of the mystery of the Trinity; three distinct polyphonic lines forming one music was a sonic/musical image of the relation of the Divine Persons constituting the one God.

I suspect that only those who had some classical musical training could have fully appreciated that what the organist was offering that Sunday morning was a sonic homily, a theological reflection on the first reading executed purely in sound without a verbal component. Although our instinct is to consider the verbal images of God proposed to us in our liturgical songs first of all, we might spend some time at least raising for ourselves the possibility of imaging God by purely musical means. I offer two further examples—one from the Gregorian chant tradition and one from Lutheran heritage.

"Gloria in excelsis" from Mass IV [2]

Anyone who has spent time analyzing the form of the "Gloria in excelsis" found in the Roman Rite recognizes that there is a slight disconnect between the theological affirmation of the equality of the Divine Persons and the amount of language devoted to each in the text. There is some debate about the addressee of the five verbs of praise and thanksgiving (*laudamus, benedicimus, adoramus, glorificamus, gratias agimus*) appearing toward the beginning of the text: Are they addressed to the Triune God (as would be suggested by the opening phrase that contrasts glory ascribed to God with peace ascribed to human beings on whom God's favor rests) or are they addressed to God the Father (as would appear from the titles *Domine Deus*, *Rex caelestis*, and *omnipotens* surrounding the following *Deus Pater*)? No matter one's decision on this, it is clear that the verbiage addressed to God the Son is extensive: appositive phrase epithets, three requests, and three declarations of Jesus Christ's unique status. Contrast this with the single prepositional phrase *cum Sancto Spiritu* toward the end of the hymn. Clearly the three Divine Persons, declared dogmatically as "equal in majesty and worship" are not equally lauded in this hymn text.

In the light of this, what the anonymous composer of the chant for the "Gloria in excelsis" from Mass IV in the *Liber Usualis* did is especially interesting. [See Ex. 1] A distinctive four-note phrase followed by a six-note melisma appears on the first syllables of *Deus Pa[-ter]*, *Jesu Chris[-te]* (twice), and *Sancto Spi[-ritus]* and nowhere else in the composition. (The settings

62 The Heart of Our Music

Ex. 1

4.
x. c.

Gló-ri- a in excélsis Dé- o.   Et in térra pax ho-mí-ni-bus bónae vo-luntá- tis. Laudámus te.   Bene-dí-cimus te.   Ado-rá-mus te. Glo-ri-ficá- mus te.   Grá-ti- as ágimus tí-bi propter mágnam gló-ri-am tú- am. Dómi-ne Dé-us, Rex caeléstis, Dé-   us Pá-   ter omní-pot-ens. Dómine Fí-li   uni-géni-te Jé- su Chrí-   ste. Dómi-ne Dé-us,   Agnus Dé-i,   Fí- li-us Pá-   tris.   Qui tól-lis peccá-ta múndi, mi-se-ré-re nó-bis. Qui tóllis peccá-ta múndi,   súscipe depreca-ti-ónem nóstram. Qui sé-des ad déxteram Pátris, mi-se-ré-re nó-bis.   Quó-ni- am tu

[Musical notation: chant with text]

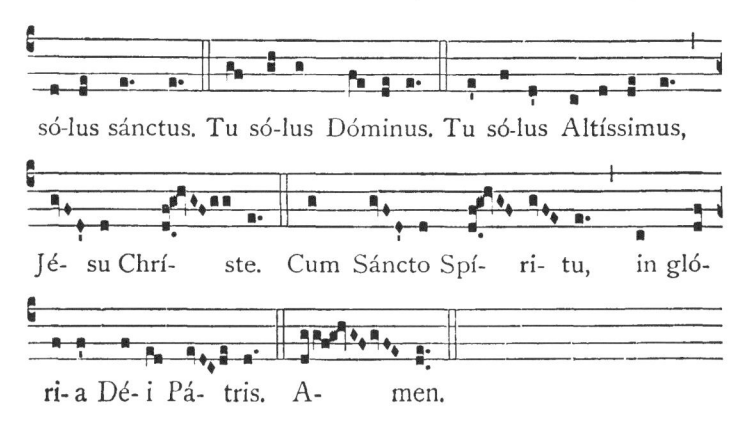

só-lus sánctus. Tu só-lus Dóminus. Tu só-lus Altíssimus, Jé- su Chrí- ste. Cum Sáncto Spí- ri- tu, in gló- ri- a Dé- i Pá- tris. A- men.

The Liber Usualis, ed. the Benedictines of Solesmes (Tournai: Desclee, 1961), 26–27. Available at http://imslp.org.

of the following syllables in these three words share a melodic curve and all cadence on the same note, but the number of notes varies, partially because the composer includes *omnipotens* within the melodic phrase after *Pater*.) It is as easy to discern this composer's intent as it is to trace a Wagnerian leitmotiv: by means of this cascade of notes applied only to the names of the Divine Persons the composer wants us to recognize that they are coequally to be worshiped, even if not in the number of words given them in the hymn.

J. S. Bach: "Gloria Patri" from Magnificat in D, BWV 243[3]

The most awe-inspiring construction of sonic/musical images for the Triune God that I have found occurs in the "Gloria Patri" movement that concludes J. S. Bach's Magnificat in D, BWV 243. [Ex. 2] The first half of the movement concentrates on the Triune God considered "in Godself": *Gloria Patri, gloria Filio, gloria et Spiritui Sancto* ("Glory to the Father, glory to the Son, and glory to the Holy Spirit"). Bach's task is to find a sonic/musical code to show the three Divine Persons one in the Godhead, differentiated as Persons and yet one. Though scored in

D major, the movement begins with the five-part chorus accompanied by woodwinds and strings singing *Gloria* on a block A major chord, the dominant of the key. Bass, tenor, alto, second soprano, and first soprano in turn then layer ascending scale passages in triplets of A major to the first syllable of *Gloria* until block B7 chords on its last two syllables, leading to a cadence on *Patri* with block chords in E major. First soprano, second soprano, alto, tenor, and bass in turn layer ascending scale passages in triplets of E major on the first syllable of *Gloria*, leading block F# 7 chords on its last two syllables, and a cadence on *Filio* with block chords in B minor. Again triplet patterns are sent through the first soprano, second soprano, tenor, alto, and bass lines in order on the first syllable of *Gloria*, but rather than ascending scale passages the voices cascade in patterns of alternating high/low/high pitches basically outlining a B minor chord, leading to block D7 chords (now accompanied by brass and timpani) on its last two syllables as well as *et Spi-*, followed by block G major chords on *ri-tu-*, block E minor chords on *i"* block A major, D major, B minor 7, and E7 chords on *San-*, concluding with a powerful cadence in A major on *-cto*.

I contend that Bach here depicts the inner Trinitarian relations by purely sonic means. Although a time signature is given, this material is performed with much *rubato*, as though time itself bows before the eternity proper to the Triune God. God the Father is sonically imaged as the fountainhead of all by means of the scale passages ascending in order through the voices from the generative bass note A. God the Son is sonically imaged as the mirror of God the Father by reversing the order of the voices' entries in their next set of ascending scale passages, the sonic equivalent of "descending from the heavens" to be born on earth. It is probably also significant that the cadence here is B minor, suggesting that the glory of the Son is found in his incarnate obedience to God the Father through his Passion and Death on the Cross. Finally the Holy Spirit is sonically imaged as the love that dances between Father and Son through the high/low/high triplet pattern marking the successive voice entrances; by

Ex. 2

66 The Heart of Our Music

Magnificat von J. S. Bach, ed. Herman Roth (Leipzig: C. F. Peters, 1910), 48–49. Available at http://imslp.org.

cadencing on A major, Bach not only brings the key relations full circle (A major → A major), imaging the "self-contained" character of inner trinitarian life, but pushes the listener to anticipate a return to D major in the final half of the movement, much as God the Holy Spirit inspires human beings to enter effectively into the transformation of history.

The second half of the movement sets the second half of the Doxology: *sicut erat in principio, et nunc, et semper, et in saecula saeculorum. Amen* ("as it was in the beginning, is now, and will be forever. Amen."). Here Bach's challenge is to find a way to depict the Triune God distinct from but genuinely interacting with the created order of time and space. He does so with a series of strategies. First, unlike the *rubato*—free meter of the first half of the movement—the second half strictly follows the time signature, imaging a shift from the eternity in which the Divine Persons live to the world of time and history in which we exist. Second, in a typical example of Bach's high humor, he sets the words *Sicut erat in principio* ("As it was in the beginning") to the selfsame motifs that opened the entire composition eleven movements earlier on the word *Magnificat*. Third, to convey the fleeting instant of "now," Bach sets the word *nunc* on a single eighth note downbeat followed by two and a half beats of silence, effectively isolating "now" from the flow of time. Finally, Bach brilliantly conveys the step-by-step character of human history by having the syllable *lo-* of *saeculorum* ("of the ages") held for up to six of the eight bars given to this word in the various choral voices.

I hope my examples show how composers may provide purely sonic/musical images to convey something of the Christian theological insight into the Triune God, both "in Godself" and in relation to the created order.

Verbal/Textual Images

However powerfully sonic/musical images of God may operate in our liturgical music, verbal/textual images are probably more immediately accessible for reflection. Certainly new language addressing and describing God can found in the texts of vernacular liturgical songs developed since the Second Vatican Council. In part this new language capitalized on a new appreciation of the variety of divine images provided in the scriptural and liturgical heritage, but in part it also responded to criticism of "exclusive language" occurring both "horizontally" (the categories by which human beings were linguistically designated) and "vertically" (the categories by which the divine was linguistically designated) in texts spoken and sung in vernacular worship. "Horizontal" texts were examined for potentially offensive or damaging connotations (e.g., "one deaf and dumb" vs. "a deaf and mute human being") and the use of the masculine generic to refer to all humans. "Vertical" texts were explored for alternatives to the use of "Father" and "Son" to designate the first two Divine Persons, while "Holy Spirit" was preferred over "Holy Ghost." These new verbal/textual images for God generated much critique, both positive and negative. Some communities experimented with alternatives to Father/Son/Holy Spirit language in triads such as Creator/Redeemer/Sanctifier (strongly criticized since these titles based in function did not articulate the relations of the Divine Persons and could lead to a modalist understanding of the Triune God), *Abba/Yeshua/Hokmah* or *Sophia* (while each of these Aramaic/Hebrew terms has the advantage of appearing in the Bible and refers to persons rather than functions, *Abba* is a title, while *Yeshua* is a name and *Hokmah* or *Sophia* ["Wisdom"] could be interpreted either way, thus also obscuring the relation between the Divine Persons) and Begettor/Begotten/Breathed (rejected because, although the relations of the Divine Persons were articulated, the personal quality of these relationships was not).

In 2006 the United States Conference of Catholic Bishops approved a Directory for Music and the Liturgy for Use in the Dioceses of the United States that directly addresses the issue of verbal/textual images of God appropriate to Roman Catholic worship.[4] Two of the three "characteristics of liturgical songs" adduced by the document—doctrinal soundness, scriptural and liturgical basis, and relative fixity in number—concern the present discussion. Under the heading "Liturgical Songs Should Be Doctrinally Correct" the bishops note: "The theological adequacy of liturgical songs may be judged in two ways: [1] Individual songs should be consonant with Catholic teaching and free from doctrinal error; and [2] [t]he repertoire of liturgical songs in any given Christian community should reflect the full spectrum of the Catholic faith."

Declaring that "to be suitable for use in the Liturgy, a sung text must not only be doctrinally correct, but must in itself be an expression of the Catholic faith" and warning against certain "tendencies toward doctrinal compromise in individual songs," they declare (among other things) that in individual liturgical songs "the Doctrine of the Blessed Trinity should never be compromised through the consistent replacement of masculine pronominal references to the three Divine persons."

Turning to the issue how a liturgical music repertoire must express the fullness of the Christian mystery, the bishops note that "the use of songs doctrinally sufficient in and of themselves does not at the same time ensure the theological integrity of an entire liturgical repertoire. Every sung liturgical repertoire should include songs about the Trinity lest this most fundamental of doctrines be compromised. Hymns in every repertoire should emphasize the centrality of Christ in salvation history and reflect on his uncompromised divinity as well as on his full humanity." No explicit statements about images appropriate for liturgical singing about the Holy Spirit appear in this section.

Under the heading "Liturgical Songs Should Be Chiefly Based in the Scriptural and the Liturgical Texts" the bishops cite both *Liturgiam Authenticam* and *Sacrosanctum Concilium* to the effect that "liturgical songs in the vernacular are best drawn from Sacred Scripture or from the liturgical patrimony."

It remains to be seen how these prescriptions will assist text writers, composers, music directors, and worshipers in crafting a repertoire of liturgical music whose images of God remain both faithful to the heritage and exploratory of how God is revealing Godself in the contemporary world.

God the Father

The limited length of this essay makes it impossible to do more than sketch the biblical and liturgical heritage grounding our liturgical songs imaging God. Unlike the "gods and goddesses" of their neighbors, the God of the Hebrew people was neither a personification of the forces of nature nor an idealization of their communal values. Rather God was a living personality deeply involved in their history, revealing Godself to individuals and clans ("God of Abraham, Isaac, Jacob"), properly titled as *Elohim* ("Majesties"), *El Shaddai* ("Mountain God," "High Breasted One"), *El Elyon* ("God Most High"), or *El Olam* ("Eternal God"), and whose personal name revealed in the narrative of Exodus 3 was YHWH: "I am who I am" (Absolute Being), "I will be who I will be" (Absolute Freedom), and "I will be there for you" (Absolute Commitment) all at once. Gradually the Hebrew people came to see YHWH not only as their tribal god but as a universal God who brought all things into being, sustained and guided all through time, and in whose hands was the future. They also gradually began to think of YHWH interacting with them and with their world through "aspects" of Godself, conceptualizing them as Spirit (*ruah*), Word (*dabar*), and Wisdom (*hokmah*).

From the New Testament record, Jesus seems to have addressed God as *Abba*, a word that combines the idea of a child's intimacy with a male parent with the honor and respect an adult human gives to a patriarch (see Mark 14:36). Some of his followers also used this term to address God, implicitly claiming a share in their relationship (see Rom 8:15; Gal 4:6). In a certain sense the contemporary disputes over the proper imagery for the Abba-God of Jesus center on whether one thinks of *Abba* as a proper name (thus replacing YHWH for Christians) or a title. If it is a proper name, then Christians are to respect and reproduce

Jesus' usage even at the cost of furthering patriarchal ideas of the divine; if it is a title, it may be supplemented by other titles, though it may be accorded a certain priority.

Verbal/textual images of God the Father in the liturgical heritage are both extensive and restricted—extensive, insofar as the Old and New Testaments with their manifold verbal/textual images of God are read and sung in liturgical settings; restricted, insofar as certain images are favored, often repeated, and become standard. For example, although we read in the third-century Apostolic Tradition a stereotyped conclusion to prayer offered "to the Father, through the Son, in the Holy Spirit in the holy Church," this formula seems to have changed among orthodox believers in combating Arianism and Macedonianism in order to emphasize the equality of the three Divine Persons: "Glory to the Father, and to the Son, and to the Holy Spirit." While the liturgical year in the Roman Rite recognizes many solemnities of the Lord Jesus and acknowledges others associated with the Holy Spirit, there is no liturgical solemnity of God the Father. Nevertheless, the collects of the Roman Rite favor addressing God the Father simply as *Deus* ("God"), frequently modified by adjectives (*omnipotens et sempiterne* ["almighty and eternal"] being the most common) and sometimes specified by a relative clause stating a divine characteristic or action. The Preface of the Holy Trinity is especially rich in divine images:

> It is truly right and just, our duty and our salvation,
> always and everywhere to give you thanks,
> Lord, holy Father, almighty and eternal God.
>
> For with your Only Begotten Son and the Holy Spirit
> you are one God, one Lord:
> not in the unity of a single person,
> but in a Trinity of one substance.
>
> For what you have revealed to us of your glory
> we believe equally of your Son
> and of the Holy Spirit,
> so that, in the confessing of the true and eternal Godhead,

you might be adored in what is proper to each Person,
their unity in substance,
and their equality in majesty.

Vernacular Christian hymnody in the West has traditionally shown a reticence similar to the Roman Rite euchological tradition when addressing or describing God the Father. However, Thomas Olivers's eighteenth-century paraphrase of the Yigdal beautifully explores the Jewish scriptural heritage for images Christians apply to God the Father:

The God of Abraham praise,
Who reigns enthroned above;
Ancient of Everlasting Days,
And God of love. . . .

The God who reigns on high
The great archangels sing,
And "Holy, Holy, Holy!" cry,
"Almighty King!"
Who was, and is, the same,
And evermore shall be:
Eternal Father, great I AM,
We worship thee.

Based on 1 Timothy 1:17, Walter Chalmers Smith's nineteenth-century hymn also gathers scriptural imagery for God the Father. Although the opening stanza might lead one to think that the text is addressed to the Triune God, the final stanza makes it clear that it is addressed to the First Person of the Blessed Trinity:

Immortal, invisible, God only wise,
In light inaccessible hid from our eyes,
Most blessed, most glorious, the Ancient of Days,
Almighty, victorious, thy great name we praise. . . .

Great Father of glory, pure Father of light,
Thine angels adore thee, all veiling their sight.

All praise we would render: O help us to see
'Tis only the splendor of light hideth thee.

From the mid-twentieth century, however, vernacular hymn-writers have gone beyond the perceived cultural prejudices of biblical language to explore more far-reaching sets of images. Brian Wren has especially dedicated himself to crafting biblically and theologically informed texts that provoke reflection on the language and images we employ in addressing and describing God. The following reworking of a trinitarian doxology is typical, especially in its mix of gendered referents applied to God:

Hallelujah, Living God,
She Who Is, Blessed Be He,
Holy One of Israel!

Hallelujah, Living God,
She Who Is, Blessed Be He,
touched and seen in Jesus!

Hallelujah, Living God,
She Who Is, Blessed Be He,
loving, living Spirit!

Hallelujah, Living God,
She Who Is, Blessed Be He,
Hallelujah! Amen![5]

It should be clear that the USCCB's document cited above would not find such a text appropriate for Roman Rite liturgical worship.

Even more daring is the explicit repudiation of some of the earlier divine imagery found in the liturgical music heritage of the church in Huub Oosterhuis's "Song at the Foot of the Mountain":

You for whom no name can be found,
no path to reach your distant ground,
no word exists to praise you.
Nowhere enthroned in splendor bright,

your light remains in cloud and night,
as though one dead we find you.
You come, we know not day nor hour,
you pass us by, a dwindling fire,
no voice through forest streaming,
call from afar or voice so near,
you are not everywhere, not here,
no god born of our dreaming.

No path secure to lead the way,
no leg to stand on—where to stay?—
no rock, no firm foundation.
No streams from rock through desert flow,
no fount of blood, no heart aglow,
no soul for contemplation.
No golden precepts carved in stone,
no final judgment to be known,
in cold and frightful fashion.
You are these people, maimed and small,
nameless, deprived, yet human, all
who long to find compassion.

You, silent call from far and near,
if you exist, if you are here,
be there within their longing.
If you are not and cannot be,
illusive name, resound in me,
no god for our adoring.
You know me well, you hold me fast,
and I will name you till the last,
I call you sister, brother.
How could we live as "I" and "you,"
homeless, ignored, despairing too,
and still not know each other?[6]

I suspect many worshiping communities would balk at singing this text (especially since it is cleverly set to a variant of *Lasst Uns Erfreuen*, a tune usually associated in the English-speaking world with the text "Ye Watchers and Ye Holy Ones"). Nevertheless for those who are haunted by God's mysterious absence–

presence and who live in the "to and fro / between yes and no" (to use another of Oosterhuis's phrases) this is a profound act of faith, "hoping against hope" (Rom 4:18) that what we cling to in faith will be revealed as true.

God the Son

We now turn to the much more extensive imagery proposed for the Second Person of the Blessed Trinity in our liturgical song. The characteristic New Testament Christian faith profession ("Jesus [the] Christ is Lord!") combines the proper name of the historical Jesus (*Yehoshua/Yeshua* ["YHWH saves"], the name of Moses' right-hand man) with two titles: *Christos*, the Greek form of the Hebrew title *Mashiakh* ("Messiah"; "Anointed One"), and *Kyrios* ("Lord"; "Sovereign"). This kerygmatic formula thus combines characteristically Jewish and Greco-Roman verbal/textual images to declare belief in and commitment to Jesus. While *theos* ("God") is normally used in the New Testament to refer to the Abba-God of Jesus, there are three undisputed statements in which Jesus is called *theos* (Heb 1:8-9; John 1:1; John 20:28) and a further possible five statements in which he is designated *theos* (Rom 9:5; John 1:18; Titus 2:13; 2 Pet 1:1; 1 John 5:20). Further New Testament titles include: prophet, son of man, son of God, lamb of God, king of kings, king of the Jews, *rabboni*/rabbi, Emmanuel, apostle, *paraclete*/advocate, mediator, bridegroom, high priest, head of the church, *logos* ("word"; "template"; "order"), *eikon* ("image") of the invisible God, and so on. The short praise formulae (doxologies, eulogies, thanksgivings) in the New Testament letters are especially important in showing that Christian believers gradually came to apply to Jesus the ascriptions that had been proper to YHWH alone. Perhaps surprisingly, significant contributions to New Testament Christology were made by the liturgical hymns sung by early Christians whose texts are recorded—for example, Colossians 1:15-20; Ephesians 1:3-14; 1 Timothy 3:16; Revelation 5:9-14; 7:10; 19:6-8, and especially in the "kenosis" hymn of Philippians 2:6-11 and the *logos* hymn embedded in John 1:1-18.

Just as it is sometimes difficult to determine who the addressee of a given New Testament doxology might be—the Abba-God of Jesus or Jesus himself—it is sometimes difficult to determine the addressee of later liturgical prayer as well, the attributes of the Triune God and the attributes of Christ being shared. Although the *Kyrie eleison* litany in the Roman Rite Mass (three *Kyrie* ["Lord"] invocations followed by three *Christe* ["Christ"] invocations concluded by three *Kyrie* ["Lord"] invocations) was most primitively addressed entirely to God the Son, tropes added to the text in the Middle Ages on occasion turned the text into a Trinitarian composition, with the first three invocations directed to God the Father and the last three to God the Holy Spirit. The Eastern Trisagion hymn (*Hagios ho theos, Hagios ischyros, Hagios athanatos, eleison hemas* ["Holy God, Holy (and) mighty, Holy (and) deathless, have mercy on us"]) could easily be addressed entirely to the Triune God or each of its invocations could be addressed to one of the Divine Persons. Great controversy ensued, however, when Peter the Fuller added "who was crucified for us" between "deathless" and "have mercy." While this may be interpreted in a perfectly orthodox way, it may also be interpreted in a Theopaschite sense—that is, declaring that the divine nature (and not simply the human nature of Christ) actually *suffered*. To check this heterodox interpretation, Calandion of Antioch inserted "Christ, King" to this expanded formula, producing an unambiguously Christic hymn: "Holy God, Holy Mighty One, Holy Deathless One, Christ, King, who was crucified for us, have mercy on us."

Unlike the reticence shown by the liturgical tradition in offering verbal/textual images for God the Father, the various aspects of the Incarnation and Paschal Mystery of Christ dominate the liturgical year, its presidential prayers, and its hymnody. For example, the following sixth-century Ambrosian hymn, restored to its original form in the present *Liturgy of the Hours* from the form altered under Urban VIII and in use from 1629 until 1972, offers rich imagery in exploring the mystery of the enfleshment of God the Son:

> *Christe Redemptor omnium,*
> *Ex Patre Patris Unice,*
> *Solus ante principium*
> *Natus ineffabiliter:*

> Christ, Redeemer of all things,
> The Father's Only[-Begotten coming forth] from
>   the Father,
> Alone before the beginning
> Born beyond all ability of speech to describe it:

> *Tu lumen, Tu splendor Patris,*
> *Tu spes perennis omnium;*
> *Intende quas fundent preces*
> *Tui per orbem famuli.*

> You, the light, you, the splendor of the Father,
> You, the eternal hope of all things,
> Be attentive to the prayers which your household slaves
> Pour out throughout the world.

> *Salutis auctor, recole*
> *Quod nostri quondam corporis,*
> *Ex illibata Virgine*
> *Nascendo, formam sumpseris. . . .*

> Source of salvation, remember
> That, being born
> Of the spotless Virgin,
> You once assumed the form of our body. . . .

The Easter Sequence is similarly replete with images evoking the paschal mystery:

> *Victimae paschali laudes immolent Christiani.*
> Christians, to the Paschal Victim
>   Offer your thankful praises!

> *Agnus redemit oves*:
> A Lamb the sheep redeems;

> *Christus innocens Patri reconciliavit peccatores.*
> Christ, who only is sinless,
> Reconciles sinners to the Father.
>
> *Mors et vita duello conflixere mirando:*
> Death and life have contended in that combat stupendous
>
> *Dux vitae mortuus, regnat vivus.*
> The Prince of life, who died, reigns immortal.

If pre-Vatican II liturgical hymnody tended to concentrate on securing the divinity of Christ, contemporary vernacular hymnody tends to concentrate on securing the humanity of Jesus. Dutch poet Huub Oosterhuis's "Song of the Lord's Appearance" contemplates the mystery of the incarnation in a distinctly contemporary way:

> . . . God has no other sign, no other
> Light in our darkened world to give
> Than this man, Christ, to be our brother,
> A God in whom we all can live.
> God has revealed to every nation
> His love for us in Christ our Lord!
> In him all flesh may see salvation
> And earth be made new in God's own Word!
> The promised one of Israel's story,
> The bridegroom clad in fire and light,
> The morning sun in all its glory
> Dispelling darkness and the night
> Has come to dwell with us forever
> Uniting us in peace and love,
> And in his body we need never
> Be parted from our God above.[7]

The same author's "Song to Jesus Christ" probes the paschal mystery with parallel acuity:

> You passed this way, you came as fire throughout the night.

> Sparks glow within your name, our hearts have seen
>   your light.
> On this, our broken world, your word hangs, frayed
>   and torn,
> laid bare for us, unfurled, a mantle, draped and worn.
>
> You passed this way, you are as footprint on the sea;
> why have you gone so far, too much were you for me!
> You are eternal, true, concealed in God as breath;
> no silence speaks of you, no thought could bear your
>   death.
>
> You passed this way, once seen, a stranger known by sight,
> a fragment of our being, a friend, a glimpse of light.
> Your light, my endless song, flows in my blood as day;
> I hope, my whole life long, to greet you on the way.[8]

God the Holy Spirit

Turning finally to images of the Holy Spirit in liturgical songs, we have already noted that the Hebrew Scriptures use *ruah* ("wind"; "breath") as a quasi-personification of an aspect of God, denoting his mysteriousness, invisibility, unpredictability, and power. The Greek *pneuma* translates *ruah* in the New Testament. Jesus' act of breathing on his disciples on Easter evening (John 20:19-23) symbolically reenacts the *ruah* that YHWH blew over the primordial waters as a precedent for the "new creation" he is fashioning through his followers. Nowhere in the New Testament is the "Spirit of God" (understood as God the Father) or the "Spirit of Jesus" called *theos* or conceptualized as a distinct Divine Person.

Unlike the prayer and hymn texts describing the Triune God and the first two Divine Persons of the Blessed Trinity, liturgical sources and songs depicting the Holy Spirit develop relatively late in the Roman Rite. Ascribed to the Carolingian monk-poet Rabanus Maurus (776–856), the hymn *Veni Creator Spiritus* positively revels in the rich imagery associated with the third Divine Person:

Qui diceris Paraclitus,
Altissimi donum Dei,
Fons vivus, ignis, caritas,
Et spiritalis unctio.

You who are called the Paraclete
Gift of God Most High,
Living fountain, fire, charity,
And spiritual anointing.

Tu septiformis munere,
Digitus paternae dexterae,
Tu rite promissum Patris,
Sermone ditans guttura.

You, seven-fold by responsibility,
Finger of the Father's right hand,
You, properly the promise of the Father,
Giving speech to the tongue-tied.

The thirteenth-century "Golden Sequence," appointed in the Roman Rite to be sung on Pentecost, boasts a similar riot of images:

Veni, pater pauperum,
veni, dator munerum
veni, lumen cordium.

Come, Father of the poor!
Come, source of all our store!
    Come, within our bosoms shine.

Consolator optime,
dulcis hospes animae,
dulce refrigerium.

You, of comforters the best;
You, the soul's most welcome guest;
    Sweet refreshment here below.

In labore requies,
in aestu temperies
in fletu solatium.

> In our labor, rest most sweet;
> Grateful coolness in the heat;
> > Solace in the midst of woe.
>
> *O lux beatissima. . . .*
>
> O most blessed Light divine. . . .

Just as it has expanded the imagery associated with the Triune God and the first two Divine Persons, so contemporary vernacular hymnody is extending the images we employ for the Holy Spirit. In "Spirit of God within Me," for example, Timothy Dudley-Smith devotes a stanza each to the "Spirit of God," the "Spirit of truth," and the "Spirit of love" within the worshipers, concluding with this stirring combination of images:

> Spirit of life within me,
> possess this life of mine;
> come as the wind of heaven's breath,
> come as the fire divine!
> Spirit of Christ, the living Lord,
> reign in this house of clay,
> till from its dust with Christ I rise
> to everlasting day.[9]

Conclusion

I would like to give the final word in these short reflections on images of God in our liturgical music to Rory Cooney, an American composer who has consistently struggled to craft texts informed by sound biblical and liturgical scholarship paired to music alive to the echoes of transcendence in his culture. (And, incidentally, he has also contributed an essay to the present collection.) The concluding verse of "O Agape," a hymn that the composer is still shaping, strikes me as admirably fulfilling what the USCCB has prescribed in its Directory while also allowing genuine artistry the room to encounter the "God Beyond All Names" from Bernadette Farrell's hymn invoked above.

The earlier verses of "O Agape" follow the *via negativa*, unmasking the "idols made of stone . . . gold . . . human wealth; the idle promise . . . spoken to the most distressed; . . . the god of war." But just as Bernadette Farrell's hymn follows a deeply Catholic instinct, this lyric concludes in the *via positiva*, evoking the experience of God in a cascade of biblical images meshed with the Spirit-inspired work of the worshiping community. Best of all, the hymn-text invites us to new appreciation of the Triune God who is Agape-Love as 1 John 4:8, 16 declares, manifest in and as the *Abba* of Jesus; the Abba's Son, our brother and Savior, Jesus the Christ; and the living Wisdom of God, arising in the *Abba* and proclaimed and embodied in Jesus.

> I know you in your sacred word,
> In shepherd, gate, and mustard seed,
> In Good Samaritan,
> Lost coins and sheep and sons,
> In lily, sparrow, wheat and weeds.
> In healing hands, in those who work
> In field and mill 'til all be fed,
> We keep your memory
> In solidarity
> By sharing cup and breaking bread.
>
> *Refrain*: O agape, love freely poured,
> O Abba, mirrored in the Son,
> Sophia, flowing through the world,
> Be known in me, be known in us.[10]

Notes

1. Bernadette Farrell, "God, Beyond All Names" (Portland, OR: OCP, 1990).

2. The Christus Rex website provides both a sound recording (with organ accompaniment) and a score of the "Gloria in excelsis" from Mass IV at: http://www.christusrex.org/www2/cantgreg/kyriale_eng.

3. Public domain scores of this composition may be found at the Petrucci Music Library section of the International Music Score Library Project at: http://imslp.org/. A performance of this movement conducted by Nicholaus Harnoncourt is found at http://www.youtube.com/watch?v=ejOaUn0Ub5o&fmt=18.

4. At the time of this writing, the document has not yet received the official *recognitio* by the Congregation for Divine Worship and the Discipline of the Sacraments, but the bishops' conference teaching has been made part of the public domain. Information about this document may be found in J. Michael McMahon, "Establishing Criteria for Liturgical Songs: The Directory for Music and Liturgy," *Pastoral Music*, August/September 2007.

5. Brian Wren, "Hallelujah, Living God" (Carol Stream, IL: Hope, 2002).

6. Huub Oosterhuis, "Song at the Foot of the Mountain," © 1971, Gooi en Sticht, Bv. Baarn, The Netherlands. Exclusive Agent for English-language Countries: OCP, 5536 NE Hassalo, Portland, OR 97213. All rights reserved. Used by permission.

7. Huub Oosterhuis, "Song of the Lord's Appearance," © 1967, Gooi en Sticht. © 1981, 1982, Jan Michael Joncas Trust. Published by OCP, 5536 NE Hassalo, Portland, OR 97213. All rights reserved. Used by permission.

8. Huub Oosterhuis "Song to Jesus Christ," © 1971, Gooi en Sticht. Exclusive Agent for English-language Countries: OCP, 5536 NE Hassalo, Portland, OR 97213. All rights reserved. Used by permission.

9. Taken from "Spirit of God Within Me" by Timothy Dudley Smith. © 1968 Hope Publishing Company, Carol Stream, IL 60188, www.hopepublishing.com. All rights reserved. Used by permission.

10. Rory Cooney, unpublished lyrics. Copyright © 2008, Rory Cooney. Used with permission.

Contributors

Tony Barr is an accomplished composer of both liturgical music and poetry, as his work has been published widely in the United Kingdom, Australia, Canada, and the United States. He has served as music director for multiple parishes in the Archdioceses of Portland, Chicago, and Westminster (England), and he served for several years as director of the St. Thomas More Centre for Pastoral Liturgy in London. He taught himself Dutch in the 1960s in order to translate the liturgical poetry of Huub Oosterhuis. He has worked in several capacities with Oregon Catholic Press, and he is the co-author of *The Death of a Christian*, rev. ed., a commentary on the Order of Christian Funerals (Liturgical Press, 1991).

Rory Cooney has been director of liturgy and music at St. Anne Catholic Community in Barrington, Illinois, since 1994. His work has been published and anthologized since 1975, and he has fifteen collections of songs with three publishers. His current project is *Like No God We Had Imagined*, sixteen songs for the Christmas season, with GIA Publications. He is also the author of *Change Our Hearts*, a book of Lenten reflections published by Liguori Press. In 2014 he was honored as the Pastoral Musician of the Year by the National Association of Pastoral Musicians (NPM).

John Foley, SJ, received his PhD in liturgical theology from the Graduate Theological Union in Berkeley. He founded the Center for Liturgy at Saint Louis University in 1993 and served as its director for over 18 years. Fr. Foley is a well-known liturgist and composer of liturgical music (e.g., "Cry of the Poor," "One Bread One Body," "Come to the Water," "May We Praise You," "For You Are My God," "Keep Me Safe O God," "Dwelling Place"), with more than 150 liturgical hymns in print. Many of his compositions were written during his membership in "The St. Louis Jesuits," a group of renowned liturgical composers. Currently he is Artist in Residence in the Catholic Studies Program at Saint Louis University and editor of SLU's weekly web magazine *The Sunday Web Site* (liturgy.slu.edu).

Alan J. Hommerding is Senior Liturgy Publications Editor at World Library Publications, and a practicing pastoral musician. He holds graduate degrees in theology, liturgy, and music from St. Mary's Seminary and University, Baltimore, and the University of Notre Dame. He appears as a contributor and text writer in the *New Cambridge Dictionary of Hymnology,* and is an author of books and a composer of both instrumental and vocal/choral music.

Bob Hurd, a teacher, composer, and liturgist, currently teaches in the Graduate Program in Pastoral Ministries at Santa Clara University in California. His widely-used liturgical music is published by Oregon Catholic Press (OCP) and is featured in numerous hymnals in the United States, Canada, Great Britain, and Australia. In 2005 he received the Good and Faithful Servant award of the Southwest Liturgical Conference, and in 2010 he was recognized as Pastoral Musician of the Year by the National Association of Pastoral Musicians (NPM).

Paul Inwood is an internationally-known liturgist, composer, organist, author, and speaker. He is a *summa cum laude* graduate of the Royal Academy of Music in London, and he worked for several years at the St. Thomas More Center for Pastoral Liturgy, also in London. His music is sung in churches worldwide, and he is a regular contributor to liturgical and musical journals, forums, and blogs. In 2009 he was honored by the National Association of Pastoral Musicians (NPM) as their Pastoral Musician of the Year.

Jan Michael Joncas, a priest of the St. Paul–Minneapolis archdiocese, is Artist-in-Residence and Research Fellow in Catholic Studies at the University of St. Thomas, St. Paul, Minnesota. He holds degrees in Liturgical Studies from the University of Notre Dame and from the Pontifical Liturgical Institute in Rome. In 2007 he was honored by the National Association of Pastoral Musicians (NPM) with their Jubilate Deo award.

Credits

"Spirit of God Within Me" by Timothy Dudley Smith © 1968 Hope Publishing Company, Carol Stream, IL 60188, www.hopepublishing.com. All rights reserved. Used by permission.

"God Beyond All Names" © 1990, Bernadette Farrell. Published by OCP, 5536 NE Hassalo, Portland, OR 97213. All rights reserved. Used with permission.

"Hallelujah, Living God" by Brian Wren © 1999 Praise Partners Worship. All rights reserved. Used by permission.

"Song at the Foot of the Mountain," text by Huub Oosterhuis © 1971, Gooi en Sticht, Bv. Baarn, The Netherlands. All rights reserved. Exclusive Agent for English-language Countries: OCP, 5536 NE Hassalo, Portland, OR 97213. All rights reserved. Used by permission.

"Song of the Lord's Appearance," text by Huub Oosterhuis © 1967, Gooi en Sticht, Bv. Baarn, The Netherlands. © 1981, 1982, Jan Michael Joncas Trust. Published by OCP, 5536 NE Hassalo, Portland, OR 97213. All rights reserved. Used by permission.

"Song to Jesus Christ," text by Huub Oosterhuis © 1971, Gooi en Sticht, Bv. Baarn, The Netherlands. All rights reserved. Exclusive Agent for English-language Countries: OCP, 5536 NE Hassalo, Portland, OR 97213. All rights reserved. Used by permission.

The English translation of a Gospel Verse from *Lectionary for Mass* © 1969, 1981, 1997, International Commission on English in the Liturgy Corporation (ICEL); excerpts from the English translation of *The Roman Missal* © 2010, ICEL. All rights reserved.

Scripture texts in this work are taken from the *New American Bible, revised edition* © 2010, 1991, 1986, 1970 Confraternity of Christian Doctrine, Washington, D.C. and are used by permission of the copyright owner. All Rights Reserved. No part of the *New American Bible* may be reproduced in any form without permission in writing from the copyright owner.

Excerpts from the *Lectionary for Mass for Use in the Dioceses of the United States of America, second typical edition* © 2001, 1998, 1997, 1986, 1970 Confraternity of Christian Doctrine, Inc., Washington, DC. Used with permission. All rights reserved. No portion of this text may be reproduced by any means without permission in writing from the copyright owner.

Excerpts from documents of the Second Vatican Council are from *Vatican Council II: The Conciliar and Postconciliar Documents*, edited by Austin Flannery, OP, © 1996. Used with permission of Liturgical Press, Collegeville, Minnesota.